John Stalker, George Parker

A Treatise of Japaning and Varnishing

being a compleat discovery of those arts, with the best way of making all

sorts of varnish for japan, wood, prints, or pictures - the method of

guilding, burnishing, and lackering, with the art of guilding

John Stalker, George Parker

A Treatise of Japaning and Varnishing
being a compleat discovery of those arts, with the best way of making all sorts of varnish for japan, wood, prints, or pictures - the method of guilding, burnishing, and lackering, with the art of guilding

ISBN/EAN: 9783337311063

Printed in Europe, USA, Canada, Australia, Japan

Cover: Foto ©Andreas Hilbeck / pixelio.de

More available books at **www.hansebooks.com**

A

TREATISE

OF

JAPANING

AND

VARNISHING,

Being a compleat Difcovery of thofe ARTS.

WITH

The beft way of making all forts of VARNISH for
JAPAN, WOOD, PRINTS, or PICTURES.

The Method of
GUILDING, BURNISHING, and LACKERING,
with the Art of Guilding, Separating, and Refining METALS:
and of Painting MEZZO-TINTO - PRINTS.

Alfo Rules for
Counterfeiting TORTOISE-SHELL, and MARBLE, and for
Staining or Dying WOOD, IVORY, and HORN.

Together with
Above an Hundred diftinct Patterns for JAPAN - work, in
Imitation of the *INDIANS*, for *Tables, Stands, Frames, Cabinets,*
Boxes, &c.

Curioufly Engraven on 24 *large Copper-Plates.*

By *JOHN STALKER.*

OXFORD,
Printed for, and fold by the *Author* , living at the *Golden Ball* in *James's Market,*
London. in the Year MDCLXXXVIII. a

TO THE

RIHGHT HONOURABLE
And moſt ACCOMPLISH'D
Lady MARY JERMAN.

MADAM,

Though it may appear *Preſumptuous for ſo mean an Author, to Dedicate a Treatiſe that is ſo far from being Faultleſs, as this of mine is ; to a Perſon of ſo High a Quality, and ſuch an Exact Judgement as Your Ladiſhip : Yet thoſe very Conſiderations that argue this Dedication to be Preſumptuous, do at the ſame time Juſtify it, becauſe they prove it to be Neceſſary. (And I doubt not, but a Perſon of Your Ladiſhips Goodneſs, and Condeſcention, looks upon Neceſſity, as ſufficient to juſtify an Action of this Nature ; that might otherwiſe juſtly be reputed a Crime.) For the meaner the Author be, and the leſs perfect the Treatiſe, the greater neceſſity for a Powerful Protection, under the ſhelter of an Eminent Patronage. And how can ſuch a Book as this, that has nothing to recommend it, but the uſefulneſs, and truth of the Experiments it contains, be better ſecured, againſt the Cenſures of this our Critical Age we live in, then by the Patronage of a Lady, that is no leſs Eminent for her Quality, Beauty, and Vertue, then for her Incomparable Skill and Experience in the Arts that thoſe Experiments belong to, as well as in ſeveral others : For I know Your Ladiſhips Candor, Exactneſs, and Judgment to be ſuch, that if You find the matter of the Book to be uſeful, and to anſwer the teſt of Experience, You will eaſily over-look any Imperfections, that rigid Criticks, may Cenſure in the manner of propoſing it ; All which Encourages me to hope for a Gracious Acceptance of this ſmall preſent, which is offer'd to Your Ladiſhip with the greateſt ſincerity, and moſt profound reſpect, by*

MADAM,

Your Ladiſhips moſt Humble,

and moſt Obedient Servant

JOHN STALKER.

THE PREFACE

IF the Antiquity of an Art can advance its credit and reputation, this of the Pencil may juftly claim it; for although we cannot trace it from its Original, yet we find many valuable Pieces extant in time of Alexander the Great. The Grecians (who always encouraged Learning and Ingenuity) had fo great an honour for this Art , that they ordained, That Gentlemens Sons and Freeborn fhould be firft fent to a Painting-School, to learn the way to Paint and Draw Pictures, before they were inftructed in any other thing; Slaves and vulgar hands, by a perpetual Edict, were excluded from the benefit and practice of it: And laftly, it was enacted, That the Art it felf fhould be ranged in the firft degree of Liberal Sciences. After them the Romans entertainen it with great refpect and veneration ; and the Jews, though denied this Profeffion by their Law, were not wholly deftitute of Artifts ; for St. Luke (if Tradition may be credited) was a Painter, as well as Evangelift and Phyfitian, and for that reafon we honour and refpect him as our Patron and Protector.

The Civilized of all Ages have given it a kind and moft obliging reception : Candaules King of Lydia purchafed a Table , whereon the Battel of Magnetes was painted with excellent skill, for its weight in Gold; and King Demetrius, forbore taking the City of Rhodes, left in the fire and plunder of his fouldiers he fhould have loft a Picture, which he prized beyond the Conqueft of the Tovvn. Indeed, they are fo highly valued by us, that vve think them fit ornaments for our Churches and Altars. The Hollanders reckon their Eftates and Worth by their pieces of Painting, and Pictures vvith them are ready and current money : in thefe too they difcover their ingenuity, for you fhall rarely meet vvith a Dutch-joke, but in Picture. Some Femals have alfo been well pleafed with this Art, which they imagin can heighten and preferve their beauties ; Jezebels, who prefer Art to Nature, and a fordid Fucus to a native complexion ; and tis fo familiar to meet with thefe walking Pictures, that unlefs we are very circumfpect, we may be impofed upon with Ixion's fallacy, who embraced a Painted Vapour for a Goddefs. Painting will certainly make us furvive our felves, and render the fhadow more lafting than the fubftance , when the colours are laid in the right place, and by the Painters hand.

Begging the Mufes pardon, I fhould prefer a Picture to a Poem ; for the latter is narrow and fhort-liv'd, calculated to the Meridian of two or three Countries, and perhaps as many Ages ; but Painting is drawn in a character intelligible to all Mankind, and ftands not in need of a Glofs, or Commentator, tis an unchangeable and

univerfal language. Painting can decipher thofe myftical characters of our Faces, which carry in them the Motto's of our Souls,
whereby our very Natures are made legible. This comely part is
the Limners more peculiar Province; and if the beauty and proportion of it can excite our love and admiration, what regard and e-
fteem muft we referve for him, who can fo excellently defcribe both.
The Rarities of this Art were never yet fo common, as to make
them defpicable; for the world very feldom produced above one
famous Artifan at a time; this Age brought forth a Zeuxis, that
an Apelles, and the third an Angelo, as if a particular fprightly Genius was required, and they were to rife from the Phænix-afhes of
each other, or that Men were to be born Painters as well as Poets.

If we duly weigh the merits of the Pencil, we fhall find the deference and refpect which our Predeceffors paid to the Mafters of it,
was moft juft and reafonable; and that we our felves ought not to
be wanting in gratitude and addrefs. By the Painters affiftance, we
enjoy our abfent friends, and behold our deceafed Anceftors face to
face: He it is, that ftretches out our Eighty to eight Hundred
years, and equals our Age to that of our Forefathers. The Egyptian
Pyramids and embalming Spices of Arabia, were not fufficient to
refcue the Carcafs from corruption or decay; and 'twas a grand
miftake, to fuppofe the Afhes of one body could be preferved by
the duft of another: Painting only is able to keep us in our Youth
and perfection; That Magick Art, more powerful than Medæa's
charms, not only renews old age, but happily prevents grey hairs
and wrinkles; and fometimes too, like Orpheus for Euridice, forces
the fhades to a furrender, and pleads exemption from the Grave.
Mahomet's is truly the Painter's Paradife, for he alone can oblige
with a Miftrefs for ever young and blooming, and a perpetual
Spring is no where to be found but in his Landskip. In fine, what
were the Heathen Gods but fancies of the Painter, all their Dei-
ties were his handywork, and Jove himfelf ftole his boafted Immor-
tality from him.

Well then, as Painting has made an honourable provifion for our
Bodies, fo Japanning has taught us a method, no way inferior to
it, for the fplendor and prefervation of our Furniture and Houfes.
Thefe Buildings, like our Bodies, continually tending to ruin and
diffolution, are ftill in want of frefh fupplies and reparations: On
the one hand they are affaulted with unexpected mifchances, on the
other with the injuries of time and weather; but the Art of Japanning has made them almoft impregnable againft both: no damp
air, no mouldring worm, or corroding time, can poffibly deface it;
and, which is much more wonderful, although its ingredients, the
Gums, are in their own nature inflammable, yet this moft vigo-
roufly refifts the fire, and is it felf found to be incombuftible. True,
genuine Japan, like the Salamander, lives in the flames, and ftands
unalterable, when the wood which was imprifon'd in it, is utterly
confumed. Juft fo the Asbefton of the Ancients, the cloath in

which

which they wrapped the dead bodies, lay unchanged and entire on the Funeral Pile, and preferved the body, when reduced to afhes, from being mixt with common, and undiftinguifht duft.   Not that tis only ftrong and durable, but delightful and ornamental beyond expreffion : What can be more furprizing, than to have our Chambers overlaid with Varnifh more gloffy and reflecting than polifht Marble ? No amorous Nymph need entertain a Dialogue with her Glafs, or Narciffus retire to a Fountain, to furvey his charming countenance, when the whole houfe is one entire Speculum.   To this we fubjoin the Golden Draught, with which Japan is fo exquifitely adorned, than which nothing can be more beautiful, more rich, or Majeftick : Let not the Europeans any longer flatter themfelves with the empty notions of having furpaffed all the world befide in ftately Palaces, coftly Temples, and fumptuous Fabricks ; Ancient and modern Rome muft now give place : The glory of one Country, Japan alone, has exceeded in beauty and magnificence all the pride of the Vatican at this time, and the Pantheon heretofore ; this laft, as Hiftory informs us, was overlaid with pure Gold, and 'twas but proper and uniform to cloath the Gods and their Temples with the fame metal.   Is this fo ftrange and remarkable ? Japan can pleafe you with a more noble profpect, not only whole Towns, but Cities too are there adorned with as rich a Covering ; fo bright and radiant are their Buildings, that when the Sun darts forth his luftre upon their Golden roofs, they enjoy a double day by the reflection of his beams.   Thefe delights would make us call to mind the fictions of the Poets, and perfwade us that the Golden Age was ftill in being, or that Midas his Wifh had at length fucceeded.   Surely this Province was Nature's Darling, and the Favourite of the Gods, for Jupiter has vouchfaft it a Vifit, as formerly to Danae, in a Golden fhower.

The EPISTLE to the
READER and PRACTITIONER.

WE have laid before you an Art very much admired by us, and all those who hold any commerce with the Inhabitants of JAPAN; but that Island not being able to furnish these parts with work of this kind, the English and Frenchmen have endeavoured to imitate them: that by these means the Nobility and Gentry might be compleatly furnisht with whole Setts of Japan-work, whereas otherwise they were forc'd to content themselves with perhaps a Screen, a Dressing-box, or Drinking-bowl, or some odd thing that had not a fellow to answer it: but now you may be stockt with entire Furniture, Tables, Stands, Boxes, and Looking-glass-frames, of our make and design, or what fashion you please; and if done by able Hands, it may come so near the true Japan, in sweetness of Black, and neatness of Draught, that no one but an Artist should be able to distinguish 'em. 'Tis certain, that not only here, but in JAPAN too, there is a vast difference in work: we our selves have seen some that has been brought from thence, as mean and ordinary in Draught, (though the ground-work may be pretty good,) as you can possibly imagine. As for our Undertakers in this kind they are very numerous, and their works are different; some of them have more confidence than skill and ingenuity, and without modesty or a blush impose upon the Gentry such Stuff and Trash, for Japan-work, that whether 'tis a greater scandal to the Name or Artificer, I cannot determin. Might we advise such foolish pretenders, their time would be better imployed in dawbing Whistles and Puppets for the Toy-Shops to please Children, than contriving Ornaments for a Room of State. 'Twill certainly please us to hear such Ignorants blame this our Publication of an Art, that was not understood by the world: 'tis unknown, we confess, even to them, and they themselves will find upon examination, that we have discovered more than they ever knew or dreamt of, and in spite of all their Bravado's, will be beholding to our Rules and Patterns: These Pages are so far from exposing our Art, that on the contrary it enhances and raises its esteem and value. These will assist 'em to distinguish between good Work and Rubbish, between an ignorant Knave and an Artist, and put a stop to all the cheats and cousenage of those whistling, impotent fellows, who pretend to teach young Ladies that Art, in which they themselves have need to be instructed, and to the disgrace of the Title lurk and shelter themselves under the notion of Japanners, Painters, Guilders, &c.

What we have delivered in this Treatise, we took not upon Trust or Hearsay, but by our own personal knowledge and experience do promise and aver, that if you punctually observe them, you must of necessity succeed well; and if any Gentlemen or Ladies, having met with disappointments in some of the Receipts, do question the truth and reality of them, they may for their satisfaction (if it stands with their convenience) see them tried by the Author, according to the very Rules set down; who is in this, and all other Commands, their most ready and most humble Servant.

In the Cutts or Patterns at the end of the Book, we have exactly imitated their Buildings, Towers and Steeples, Figures, Rocks, and the like, according to the Patterns which the best workmen amongst them have afforded us on their Cabinets, Screens, Boxes, &c. Perhaps we have helpt them a little in their proportions, where they were lame or defective, and made them more pleasant, yet altogether as Antick. Had we industriously contriv'd a prospective, or shadow'd them otherwise than they are; we should have wander'd from our Design, which is only to imitate the true genuine Indian work, and perhaps in a great measure might puzzle and confound the unexperienced Practitioner.

We know nothing farther that wants an Apology or Explanation; but to these our Endeavours do subjoin our hearty Wishes for your happy Progress and Success, and Subscribe,

YOURS.

ERRATA.

In the Preface, page i. *line* 4. *for* in time, *read,* in the time. *l.* 20. *for* Magnetes, *read,* the Magnetes *l.* 28. *for*, better joke, *read,* better Dutch joke. *l. ult.* tis unchangeable, *read,* for tis unchangeable.

In the Book, Page 5. *line* 16. *for*, silver, *read,* silver-dull. *p.* 7. *l.* 25. *for* Smalt, *read* Lake. *l.* 45. *for* Sea-green, *read* fine Smalt, *and for*, Greens, *read,* Blews. *p.* 25. *l.* 32. *for.* Muller or, *read* Muller and *p.* 29. *l.* 47. *for,* Venice Turpentine, *read,* oyl of Turpentine. *l. ult. for* Turpentine, *read,* Turpentine-oyl *p.* 36. *after line the* 27. *read* CHAP. XIII. *p.* 60. *l* 9. *for,* narrow, *read,* many *p.* 77. *l.* 16. *for* red, *r.* brown-red. *l.* 16. *after* vermilion, *read,* or.

CONTENTS.

THE ART OF
JAPANNING, VARNISHING, &c.

EVery Artift, who undertakes to treat of his Profeffion, before he enters on the work, muft defcribe the Inftruments and Materials with which it muft be performed: and by obferving this method, thofe perfons who either for diverfion or advantage defign to be Mafters of this Art, furnifh themfelves with all things neceffary after the beft manner, fhall lay a good foundation, and may proceed to practife with chearfulnefs and fuccefs. And that no one may impofe upon you in the Price or Goodnefs of your Drugs; that your Spirits be very ftrong, your Gums and Metals of the beft; take this following account, as your only fecurity againft all coufenage and impofture. But before I fpeak of thefe things which the Shops fupply us with, I prefume tis convenient to acquaint you with others, that conduce to the compofition, mixture, and prefervation of the Varnifh, Colours, &c.

And 1. two Strainers are required, made of pretty fine Flannel or ordinary courfe Linnen, in fhape like a Tunnel, or Sugar-loaf, or a Jelly-bag that women ftrain Jellies through: one is ufeful for ftraining your white Varnifh, and the other for your Lace-varnifh, and Lackers, when you make any.

2. You muft have two Tin-tunnels; one to ufe with your Lace-varnifh, and Lacker, and the other for your white varnifh for the fame ufe.

3. You muft be furnifhed with feveral Glafs bottles, and Vials fmall and great, according to the quantities of varnifh you make or ufe; and alfo with Gally-pots of feveral fizes, to put your varnifh in when you intend to varnifh: and for your Blacks, with which other things muft fometimes be mixed, Gally-pots are better than any other veffels to mix your blacks and hold your varnifh, becaufe they are deeper than Pottingers, and not fo wide, fo that the varnifh doth not fo foon thicken, for the Spirits in a deep Gally-pot do not fo fuddenly evaporate.

4. You fhould provide feveral forts of varnifhing-tools, or Pencils, according to the greatnefs or fmalnefs of the thing you defign to work. Your varnifhing Pencils are foft, and made of Camels hair, and are of feveral prices, according to the bignefs of them: the beft that I know are fold in Blackamoor-ftreet by Clare-market, but you may have them alfo at feveral Colour-fellers in and about London, from fix-pence to half a Crown or three fhillings the Pencil.

5. You muft procure Pencils to draw with, fmall and greater, Goofe, little Goofe, Duck, and Swallow-quills, according to your

B   work.

work. The longeſt haired Pencils I eſteem the beſt for this uſe ; you may have them all at the places aforeſaid.

6. You ſhould get 200 of Muſle-ſhells, that you may have them always in readineſs to mix your Metals or Colours in, as occaſion ſhall ſerve: not that you need uſe the tenth part of them at once, but that you may not be to ſeek when you want; and for change, when your metals or colours, by frequent mixture, ſhall grow dirty, which will be, if you work in Gum-water, as I ſhall hereafter obſerve.

7. You ſhould furniſh your ſelf with Ruſhes, which are called Dutch-Ruſhes, with which you muſt ſmooth your work before you varniſh it; and as you lay your ground of Colour or Black, if any knob or roughneſs appear on your work, you muſt take a Ruſh and ruſh it off; ſo muſt you do as oft as you find any roughneſs or grittineſs upon your work, either in laying your Grounds, or varniſhing it up. You may buy them at the Iron-mongers.

8. You muſt have Tripoly to poliſh your work after it is varniſhed, which muſt be ſcraped, or finely pounded and ſifted. But of this I ſhall have occaſion to ſpeak more largely, when I come to give rules for varniſhing : you may have it at the Iron-mongers.

9. You cant be without ſtore of Linnen-rags as well coarſe as fine, with which you muſt poliſh and clear up your work, as ſhall be ſhewed hereafter.

10. You muſt have Sallet-oyl for clearing up your work, as ſhall be notified in its proper place. All theſe things every Practitioner ought to provide, as being neceſſary to his future performances.

CHAP. I.

A true Character of the beſt Spirits, Gums, Metals, &c.

To know a Strong Spirit.

TO make Varniſh you muſt have Spirit of Wine, which muſt be ſtrong, or it will ſpoyl the Varniſh, and not diſſolve your Gums, and conſequently hinder your deſign; for the ſtronger your Spirits are, the better will the Varniſh be; the Spirits only being to diſſolve the Gums, in order to make them ſpread, or lie even upon the work. After it hath performed that work, the ſooner they evaporate the better, and the higher the Spirits are drawn, the leſs flegm or watery parts are in them ; and the leſs of watery parts are in the Varniſh, the ſooner it dries, and is fit for poliſhing , is more permanent, and will come to the greater and better gloſs. But this is of little uſe now Varniſh is ſo much uſed ; for the Diſtillers have learned by practice and cuſtom to make Spirits that juſt diſſolve the gums, only it requires the longer drying   Yet theſe Spirits that
are

are commonly ufed will fometimes be too weak, either by neglect or diſhoneſty of the Diſtiller, who hath not fufficiently deflegm'd or drawn all the watery from the ſpirituous parts. Therefore the beſt way to prove your Spirits, is to take ſome in a ſpoon, and put a little Gun-powder in it, and then ſet the Spirit on fire with a little paper or candle, as you do Brandy, and if it burn ſo long till it fire the Gunpowder before it go out, it is fit for uſe, and will diſſolve your Gums. All pretenders to this Art know this way of trying Spirits, and the damage weak Spirits do the Varniſh : but ſince my deſign is to inform the ignorant and learner, it is reaſonable and neceſſary in this place to infert it.

To chooſe Gum Lac, called Seed-Lac.

The beſt Seed-Lace is that which is large-grained, bright, and clear, freeſt from duſt, ſticks, and drofs. The Drugſters afford it at ſeveral rates, proportionable to its goodneſs, generally for 14. 16. 18d. the pound.

To chooſe Gum Sandrick.

The beſt Gum-Sandrick is the largeſt and whiteſt, or that which caſts the leaſt yellow. Let it be as free from duſt or drofs as you can. The value of it is commonly 12 or 14d. the pound.

To chooſe Gum Animæ.

The whiteſt, cleareſt, and moſt tranſparent is the beſt, and the price is ſometimes 3, 4, or 5s. the pound, according to the goodne

Venice-Turpentine.

The only directions that can be given for the choice of it are, that the cleareſt, fineſt, and whiteſt is the beſt ; and is ſold at 18 or 20d. the pound.

White Roſine.

The beſt white Rofine is white and clear, and purchaſed at 4d. or 6d. the pound.

Shell-Lace.

The beſt Shell-Lace is the moſt tranſparent, and thinneſt, and that which (if melted with a candle) will draw out in the longeſt and fineſt hair (like melted wax) becauſe the tougheſt. There are counterfeits, which you muſt endeavour to difcover by the aforementioned rule. The true may be procured at 18d. or 2s. the pound.

Bole Armoniak.

The beſt Bole Armoniak is as fine as red Oker, and of a deep dark, blackiſh-red colour, free from grittineſs or gravel, and is commonly called French-Bole.

Gum Arabick.

The beſt is clear, tranſparent, and white : you may pick it your ſelf from the Drugſters, but then you muſt pay ſomething more ; the common rate is 12d. the pound.

Gum

Gum Capall.

The beſt Capall is the whiteſt, freeſt from droſs, and thick dark ſtuff that is incorporated with the Gum. It is of it ſelf a thick whitiſh heavy Gum, and rarely without that dark and droſſy mixture ; but that which is cleareſt and freeſt from the ſaid ſtuff is the beſt. The price is 12, 16, or 18d. the pound, according to the goodneſs.

To chooſe Gum Elemni.

The beſt Gum Elemni is the hardeſt, whiteſt, and cleareſt, freeſt from droſs or dirt. It is brought over commonly in the bark or huſk of a Tree ; which you may take off as well as you can before you uſe it. The Shops can afford it at 4 or 5d. the ounce.

Roſine.

The beſt is the clear, and tranſparent, and clarified. It may be had at 3d. the pound.

Iſinglaſs.

The beſt Iſinglaſs is that which is cleareſt, and whiteſt, freeſt from yellowneſs. It is, if good, worth 3 or 4d. the ounce ; you may have it cheaper by the pound. The ſame may be obſerved by other things ; for the greater quantity you buy at a time, the cheaper will your purchaſe be.

Gambogium.

The beſt is that of the brighteſt yellow, and freeſt from droſs. Some of it is dirty, thick, and full of droſs : there is difference in the price according to the goodneſs ; the beſt is worth 6d. the ounce.

To chooſe Benjamin, or Benzoine.

The beſt is that of a bright reddiſh colour, very like to clarified Roſine, but never ſo fine, freeſt from droſs or filth. Tis as in goodneſs, 4d, 6d, or 8d, the ounce.

Dragons Blood.

The beſt is the brighteſt red, and freeſt from droſs. You may buy it in drops (as the Drugſters call it) which is the beſt. They are made up in a kind of leaf or huſk : it is commonly 8d. ſometimes 12d. the ounce, according to the goodneſs.

I have here given you an account of thoſe things and Gums you will have occaſion for in Japanning and Varniſhing, and are all to be bought at the Drugſters at or neer the prizes I have ſpecified ; and may ſerve to inform you in ſome meaſure of the Gums, their excellencies and value, but time and practice will make greater diſcoveries. Indeed grains of Allowance muſt be made for their different prizes ; for their riſe and fall depends upon the plenty or ſcarcity of them, and varies according to the goodneſs of the commodity. It is not neceſſary to furniſh your ſelf with all, or any part of theſe, but as you have occaſion to make uſe of them : for of

ſome,

fome an ounce will ferve you a great while, of others a pound will be ufed at one time; of which you will know more, as I fhall have occafion to treat of them in their order. I fhall now proceed to Metals, which I will alfo give you fome account of; and firft,

Of Brafs-duft, which is commonly amongft the Artifts called Gold-duft.

This cannot be made in England fit for ufe, though it hath often been attempted, but comes from beyond Sea, as the reft of the Metals do that are good. Germany is the place where the beft of all forts is made. The beft Brafs-duft is that which is fineft, and of the brighteft and moft gold-like colour; which you may beft difcern, by taking a little on your finger, and fqueezing it along your finger with your thumb; and if it be good, it will look with a bright and rich luftre, if bad, it will appear of a dull clayifh colour, and will never work lively and bright. Several forts of this Metal are imported here from foreign parts; which differ vaftly as to the coarfnefs and finenefs, and the different ways of working them: As for inftance, the coarfer fort will work well with Gold-fize, which will not with Gum-water; other differences will arife alfo, which are fubject to the difcoveries of practice and experience. From this difference of Metals proceeds that of the prizes; for fome are worth 12 or 14s. the ounce, whilft that others amount to not above 4 or 5s. for the fame quantity. But thefe are two extremes; the firft very good, and the other altogether as vile and bad; for there is a middle fort between both, which is generally afforded, by thofe that buy of the Merchant, for 8 or 9s. the ounce, which will work well.

To choofe Silver-duft.

Some have attempted to make Silver here in England, but none I ever faw comparable to that beyond Sea; for that enjoys a lively bright luftre like polifhed or new-coined filver, (which you may find by fqueezing it between your finger and thumb) whereas that which we make here is dull, dead, and heavy, and indeed is a fitter reprefentation of a Colour than a Metal; and by comparifon you may find, how the dimnefs of the counterfeit is obfcured by the dazling luftre of the true. Its price is anfwerable to its goodnefs and excellency, for its loweft rate is no lefs than 16s. the ounce. But I would not have the price fright any one fo far, as to prefer cheaper before it, for tis neither fo ufeful nor pleafant in the work, and the beft will go farther than this proportionable to its price. Tis cuftomary in Japan to ufe feveral forts of Metals that are corrupted and adulterate, and they are layed too in garments, flowers, houfes, and the like, which makes the work look more beautiful and furprizing. thefe likewife are vended and fold for the aforefaid ufe, and are commonly called,

Firft, Green-gold,

Is a certain corrupted mettle, cafting a kind of a dead greenifh colour, and is commonly fold at 6s. the ounce.

Dirty

Dirty-Gold

Is another kind of corrupted metal, which bears some resemblance to drossy dirty Gold : it may be purchased at 6s. the ounce.

Powder-Tinn

Is Tinn grinded to dust, of a dull, dark, though silverish colour ; made use of in Rocks, &c. Its price the same with the former.

Of Coppers

There are three sorts, Natural, Artificial, and Adulterate.

The Natural is ground without mixture, well cleansed, and is of the true genuine colour of Copper, and is sold at 6 or 7s. the ounce.

The Artificial accordingly exceeds the Natural ; it is more deep and red, but very clear, and its bright glittering colour shews how far it is possible for Art to exceed Nature. Tis very rarely procured, or sold under 10s. the ounce.

The Adulterate Copper is of a thick , heavy, metallick colour, and is commonly used to work other metals on, as if that be layed for a Ground, you hatch or highten with bright gold, or other light metal ; and sold at 6s. the ounce.

There is also used in Japan-work metals , commonly called Speckles, of divers sorts, as Gold, Silver, Copper, and many other colours, some finer than other, and worked according to the fancy of the Artist, either on Mouldings, the out or in-side of Boxes, Drawers, &c.

Of these, those that are used in the Indian work, are the Gold, Silver, and Copper, though, as aforesaid, every one may take their own fancy or humor in the use of them. They are made here in England very well, and are sold each of them much at a price, 5 or 6 shillings the ounce, according as they are in fineness. So that what I said concerning the rates of Gums, will hold good here also, That a glut or scarcity of these enhances or abates the price ; but generally these are exposed to sale at the rates I have affixed to each of them. These are sold by great quantities by several Merchants in London ; and in lesser, by as many. I shall only mention two, viz. a Gold-beater, at the hand and hammer in Long-acre ; and another of the same trade, over against Mercers-Chappel in Cheapside.

Having given you an account of Gums, and Metals, I shall briefly run over the Colours, which formerly our ignorant English and French Practitioners used to mix with their Japan-work, but improperly ; for the true natural Japan-work, so called from the Island of that name, did so far surpass all the painting of Bantam, and the neighbouring places, in goodness of black and stateliness of draught, that no fidling pretender could match or imitate it ; and the ignorant undertaker not being able to make his work look well and

lively,

lively, inferts feveral colours as a file to fet it off, when (unfortunate man) inftead of art, fancy, and skill, he expofes a piece gay, queint, gawdy, finical, and mean, the genuine product of ignorance and prefumption; and an ornament of Bartholmew, or Alehoufe, rather than a Palace or Exchange. The miftake of Bantam-work for Japan, arofe from hence: all work of this kind was by a general name called Indian; by ufe they fo far confounded all together, that none but the skilful could rightly diftinguifh. This muft be alledged for the Bantam-work, that tis very pretty, and fome are more fond of it, and prefer it to the other, nay the work is equally difficult with Japan: But if I muft give you my opinion, my skill and fancy induce me to believe, that Japan is more rich, grave, and Majeftick, and for that reafon ought to be more highly efteemed. But fancy, like Proteus, putting on a thoufand fhapes, cannot, ought not, be confined; and thofe who are inclined to admire colours, may find fafe and exact rules fet down by way of information.

And firft, fome colours we call tranfparent; fuch as are thofe we lay upon Silver, Gold, or fome light colour, and then they appear in their proper colours very beautiful and lively. Of thefe for your ufe is, firft, Diftilled Verdigreece, for a green; fine Lake for a red; fine Smalt, for a blew. To render thefe ufeful, you muft obferve the following method: having provided a Porphyr, or Marble ftone, with a Muller, take what quantity of Verdigreece or Smalt you pleafe, and with Nut-oyl, fo much as will juft moiften it fit to work, grind it upon your ftone till it be as fine or finer than butter; then put them in fhells, mixing them with Turpentine-oyl till they be thin enough for your ufe, lay thefe upon filver, gold, or any other light colour, and they will be tranfparent, and alter their lightnefs or darknefs according to the lightnefs or darknefs of the metals or colours you lay under them. The fame may you do with Lake for a red, only inftead of Nut-oyl, ufe Drying oyl to grind it in.

Other colours are ufed which have a body, and are layed on the black of your table or box, where you have defigned any thing, as Flowers, Birds, &c. Thefe are Vermilion for a red, White-lead for a white; fome ufe Flake-white for a white, which is a purer white, and much better, but for ordinary work the other will do: if you make a blew to lay upon your work, you muft take Smalt, and mixing it with Gum Arabick-water put in what quantity of white-lead you pleafe, to make it deeper or lighter, as your fancy fhall direct; but you muft put in white-lead, becaufe your blew will not otherwife have a body; fo muft you do with all colours that have not a body of themfelves. Some ufe Rozett, fine Lake, and Sea-green, for a Purple, and other forts of Reds and Greens: and indeed ways of working are very numerous, which being now out of fafhion, I fhould to no purpofe both trouble you, and tire my felf, by increafing the number; thofe which I have mentioned are

abun-

abundantly sufficient, for any that design to have something beside
gawdy colours in their work. Twill be convenient here to insert a
caution concerning these Colours; that they are all to be layed
with Gum-water, except the transparent ones above-mentioned
and whosoever hath a mind to work, either in Gum-water, or Gold-
size, shall hereafter receive sufficient Instructions for both.

According to my promise I have in full treated of Gums, Metals, and Colours; I shall now in full proceed to discover the methods that are used to make Varnishes.

CHAP. II.

How to make VARNISHES.

To make Seed-Lace-Varnish.

TAke one gallon of good Spirit, and put it in as wide-mouthed a
bottle as you can procure; for when you shall afterwards
strain your varnish, the Gums in a narrow-mouthed bottle
may stick together, and clog the mouth, so that it will be no easie
task to separate or get them out. To your spirits add one pound
and a half of the best Seed-lace; let it stand the space of 24 hours,
or longer, for the Gum will be the better dissolved: observe to
shake it very well, and often, to keep the Gums from clogging or
caking together. When it hath stood its time, take another bottle of the same bigness, or as many quart-ones as will contain your
varnish; and your strainer of flannel made as aforesaid in this book,
fasten it to a tenter-hook against a wall, or some other place convenient for straining it, in such a posture, that the end of your
strainer may almost touch the bottom of your Tin-tunnel, which
is supposed to be fixed in the mouth of your empty bottle, on purpose to receive your strained varnish. Then shake your varnish
well together, and pour or decant into your strainer as much as
conveniently it will hold, only be sure to leave room for your
hand, with which you must squeez out the varnish; and when the
bag by so doing is almost drawn dry, repeat it, till your strainer being almost full of the dregs of the Gums, shall (the moisture being
all pressed out) require to be discharged of them: which fæces or
dregs are of no use, unless it be to burn, or fire your chimny. This
operation must be continued, till all your varnish is after this manner strained; which done, commit it to your bottles close stopt,
and let it remain undisturbed for two or three days: then into another clean empty bottle pour off very gently the top of your varnish, so long as you perceive it to run very clear, and no longer;
for as soon as you observe it to come thick, and muddy, you must
by all means desist: and again, give it time to rest and settle, which
'twill do in a day or two; after which time you may attempt to
draw off more of your fine varnish, and having so done you may
                                                              lay

lay it up, till your art and work shall call for its assistance. 'Tis certain, that upon any emergency or urgent occasion you may make varnish in less time than 24 hours, and use it immediately, but the other I recommend as the best and more commendable way: besides, the varnish which you have from the top of the bottles first pour'd off, is of extraordinary use to adorn your work, and render it glossy and beautiful. Some Artists, through haste or inadvertency, scruple not to strain their varnish by fire or candle-light: but certainly day-light is much more proper, and less dangerous; for should your varnish through negligence or chance take fire, value not that loss, but rather thank your stars that your self and work-house have escaped. Should I affirm, that the boiling the Lacker and Varnish by the fire, were prejudicial to the things themselves, I could easily make good the assertion; for they are as well and better made without that dangerous element, which if any after this caution will undertake, they may feelingly assure themselves that tis able to spoil both the Experiment and Operator. On the other hand, no advantage or excellence can accrue either to Lacker or Varnish; especially when, as some of them do, tis boiled to so great a height, that this Ætna is forc'd to throw out its fiery eruptions, which for certain consume the admiring Empedocles, who expires a foolish and a negligent Martyr; and it would almost excite ones pitty, to see a forward ingenious undertaker, perish thus in the beginning of his Enterprise; who might have justly promised to erect a noble and unimitable piece of Art, as a lasting monument of his fame and memory: but (unhappy man) his beginning and his end are of the same date: his hopes vanish, and his mischance shall be registred in doggrel Ballad, or be frightfully represented in a Puppet-shew, or on a Sign-post.

To make Shell-Lacc-varnish.

Whosoever designs a neat, glossy piece of work, must banish this as unserviceable for, and inconsistent with, the rarities of our Art. But because tis commonly used by those that imploy themselves in varnishing ordinary woods, as Olive, Walnut, and the like; tis requisite that we give you directions for the composition of it, that if your conveniency or fancy lead that way, you may be supplied with materials for the performance. Having therefore in readiness one gallon of the best Spirit, add to it one pound and a half of the best Shell-Lace. This mixture being well stirred and shaked together, should stand about twenty four hours before tis strained. You might have observed, that the former varnish had much sediment and dregs; this on the contrary has none, for it wholly dissolves, and is by consequence free from all dross or faeces; tis requisite however to strain it, that the sticks and straws, which often are in the Gum, may by this percolation be separated from the varnish. But although this admits of no sediment, and in this case differs from the aforementioned varnish, yet tis much inferior also to it in an-

other

other respect; That this will never be fine, clear, and transparent;
and therefore 'twill be lost labour to endeavour, either by art or
industry, to make it so. This small advantage however doth arise,
that you need not expect or tarry for the time of its perfection, for
the same minute that made it, made it fit for use. This, as I hinted before, is a fit varnish for ordinary work that requires not a
polish; for though it may be polished, and look well for the present, yet like a handsom Ladies beautiful face, it hath no security
against the injuries of time; for but a few days will reduce it to
its native mist and dulness. Your common Varnish-dawbers frequently use it, for tis doubly advantageous to them: having a
greater body than the Seed-Lace, less labour and varnish goes to
the perfecting their work; which they carelesly slubber over, and
if it looks tolerably bright till tis sold, they matter not how dull
it looks afterward; and lucre only being designed, if they can compass that, farewel credit and admiration.   Poor insufficient Pretenders, not able to make their work more apparent, or more lasting than their knavery! And tis pretty to think, that the same
misty cloak will not cover the fraud and the impostor! that the
first should be a foil to the second, and the dull foggy work serve
only to set off the knavish Artist in his most lively colours! But
to conclude, if with a pint of this varnish you mix two ounces or
more of Venice-turpentine, it will harden well, and be a varnish
good enough for the inside of Drawers, frames of Tables, Stan-pil-
lars, frames of Chairs, Stools, or the like. Painters Lacker made
also with this Varnish, and something a larger quantity of Turpentine put to it; serves very well for lackering of Coaches, Houses,
Signs, or the like, and will glofs with very little heat, and, if occasion be, without.

To make the best White-varnish.

I would defire the Reader to observe, that when any Drugs,
Gums, or Spirits, are set down for the use and making of Varnish,
Lacker, or the like, though we do not to every particular write
the best of such a sort, yet that you should understand our meaning
to be such, when we do not particularly forbid the getting or buy-
ing of the best; for tis irksom and tedious to every single drug to
affix the word Best: wherefore to avoid so needless a repetition,
I shall forbear mentioning it above once, either at the beginning or
end, as it shall seem most necessary. Besides, tis a very reasonable
suppofition; for you must not expect to raise a Noble piece from
drofs or rubbish; to erect a Louvre or Escurial with dirt or clay,
nor from a common Log to frame a Mercury. But to return to
our design of White-varnish: Being furnished with one pound of
the whitest Gum Sandrick, one ounce of the whitest Gum Maftick,
of the cleareft Venice-Turpentine three ounces, one ounce and a
half of Gum-Capal, of Gum-Elemni half an ounce, of Gum-Ben-
zoin or Benjamin the cleareft half an ounce, one ounce and half of
the cleareft Gum Animæ, and of white Rofine half an ounce. The

Gums

Gums thus separately and in their due quantities provided, each being the best and most excellent in its kind; I must desire you to observe carefully the following order in their mixture and dissolution. Put the Capal and Rosine in a glass-vial, with half a pint of Spirits to dissolve them: for the same end to another glass, containing three quarters of a pint of Spirits, confine the Gum Animæ, Benjamin, and Venice-Turpentine. The Gum Sandrick and Mastick should likewise enjoy the priviledg of a distinct bottle, and in it a pint and half of Spirits, for their more effectual dissolution; and lastly, the Gum Elemni by it self, content with one quarter of a pint of Spirits to dissolve it. Tis not highly necessary to observe the quantities of Spirits so exactly: but this in general I advise, that all your Spirits exceed not three quarts. They must in this distinct manner be dissolved, the better to extract the whole virtue of each Gum, and prevent their clogging and caking together, which would much hinder their being quickly or throughly dissolved. I must not forget further to acquaint you, that the Gum Animæ and Benjamin be very finely pounded and reduced to powder, before they are mixed with the Spirits; you may also bruise the Capal and Rosine, as for the rest, they may be used or put into the Spirit as you buy them, without any alteration. Having thus carefully mixt 'em, let them caress one another for two or three days, and make them dance or change places, by shaking very briskly each bottle or vial once in two hours for the first day; the remaining time shake them at your own conveniency. Then take a bottle large and capacious enough to hold all the varnish you have made, and through the fine linnen Strainer (of which in the beginning) strain all your gums, mixt as aforesaid; but squeez gently, and not with so close an hand as was required for your Seed-Lace: for by this easie percolation you prevent the sandy, hard, gritty stuff passing through into your varnish. Some never strain it, but with great diligence pour it off as long as twill run clear from each bottle. But if I may be a competent Judg, this is not so good a way or so convenient, for these reasons: You have not, first, so much varnish, neither can you pour it off so clear and fine as you may by straining. Again, your dregs being left in, by frequent use will fill up your vessel, and the fresh Gums will mix with the old, and slacken the melting of them, all which our method disallows of, and keeps the bottles empty, and fit for the same repeated use, without these inconveniences. The varnish thus strained having stood three or four days, (the longer the better,) pour of gently as much as will come very clear, reserving the thick and muddy part at the bottom for ordinary uses; as mixing with other varnish for black work, or to gloss the in-side of boxes, as we shall hereafter more fully discover.

To make a White-varnish much inferior to the former.

This is made out of two distinct Varnishes, the one Sandrick, the other of Mastick; of both which take the following account.

Having

Having provided three quarters of a pound of gum Sandrick, mix it with two quarts of Spirits, and having been well shaken, and stood for about two days, decant or strain it into another bottle, and reserve it for use. Take also of clean pickt Mastick the same proportion, to an equal quantity of Spirit with the former, and in every particular observe the rules for making the Sandrick, as to setting, shaking, decanting, and straining it.

Now when you design to varnish a print or any thing else with this varnish, your usual proportion for mixing them, is to add a double part of gum Mastick to a single part of gum Sandrick. As for instance: suppose the work would take up or consume three quarters of a pint of varnish; then by the foregoing rule you must put half a pint of Mastick to a quarter of a pint of Sandrick-varnish, and so accordingly in a lesser or greater quantity. And we think fit to make these varnishes severally, and so mix them, that we may have our varnish answer to our desires in softness or hardness. Now when you have set by your work for two days, you may try its qualities, if, by pressing your warm finger on it, you leave your print behind you, tis a sign that it is too soft, and a wash or two of the Sandrick will harden it: if it not only resist your touch, but hath some streaks, flaws, or cracks, like scratches, sometimes more or less, you may be sure tis too hard, and it must be remedied by a wash or two of your Mastick-varnish. Some usually dissolve these gums together, and others mix them before hand, and by so doing are not certain how their varnish will succeed; for it often happens, that some parts of each gum are softer than others, and so the contrary. Should therefore a varnished piece prove too soft, or hard, this way cannot remedy it; for to wash it again with the same, is only a repetition of the former miscarriage. These things being premised, I need not infer which way will prove the most rational, certain, and satisfactory.

To make Varnish, that shall secure your Draught, whether Gold-work, or Colour, from the injuries of Varnishing, and will give it a gloss.

Before we come to the Varnish, tis requisite to acquaint you with the manner of preparing Turpentine, which is the chiefest ingredient. Take then of good Venice-turpentine as much as you please, inclose it in a Pipkin that will hold double the quantity that you put in. Having prepared a fire that will never flame out, but burn gently and clearly, set your pot over it, but be cautious that it boil not over, thereby to prevent the firing your Turpentine and your Chimny. To this gentle boiling motion caused by the fire you must join another, and with a stick very often stir it, until you find tis rendred fit for use; which you may discover, by dropping a little of it on the ground; for when tis cold, it will crumble to powder between your fingers, if it be sufficiently boiled; and when tis brought to this pass, nothing remains but that you let it cool, and preserve it for the following composition.

Your

Your Securing-varnish requires a quarter of a pint of the finest Seed-Lace-varnish, (which is always the top of it,) and one ounce of this boiled Turpentine finely powdered; they must be both shut up close prisoners in a double glass-vial or bottle, capacious enough to contain a double quantity; which being stopt close, may be plac'd over a very gentle fire, that it may leisurely heat, thereby to forestall the danger of breaking the glass, which it is certainly past when tis exceeding hot; and in this condition keep it for some time, simpering, and smiling: then take it off, and give it vent by unstopping; so done, return the stopple shaking it well, and place it on the fire again, never discontinuing the operation; but repeat the foresaid method, till such time as your Turpentine shall be so far dissolved, that the bigness of a large Pea shall only remain visible; for that being the dross and indissoluble part, will not endure to be incorporated. Being arrived to this degree, remove your Varnish, afford it two days to cool and settle; and vouchsafe the clearer part fresh lodgings in a clean bottle, that may entertain and keep it for your future designs.

Now whatsoever you propose to be by this varnish secured, if convenience will allow, should be destined to a warm place, that it may dry the sooner; if you cannot admit of it, then give it the space of half an hour to dry between every wash; however it will gloss either way. Then take a Pencil, for great work large, and so the contrary, proportionable to your draught: with this Pencil dipt in the varnish, secure it, that is, pass it over, leaf by leaf, and sprig by sprig, not omitting to give your Rocks, Figures, &c, the like entertainment; but be sure above all, that your steddy hand never trespass upon the least part of your black or ground-work. Having run over all your draught thus, three or four times, for oftner may spoil the colour of your metal, you may rest satisfied that your undertaking (whether of Gum-water, or Gold-size) is armed against all injuries and Tarnish; and, if performed Artist-like, adds to the native lustre of the metals, with an artificial gloss more bright, durable, and surprizing.

To secure your whole piece, both Draught and Ground-work, whereby it may endure polishing, and obtain a Gloss all over, like some of the Indian performances.

Here also, as in the last, your patience must be desir'd, and before we open our Scenes, think it reasonable to give you a survey of those passages which must be transacted in the Tiring-room or Shop, before the Actors and Operators appear on the Stage. That necessary and serviceable friend, Venice-Turpentine, here also gives his attendance: who in the quantity of one pound, to three pints of water, takes up his lodging in a clean, earthen, Pipkin, almost as large again as the Inhabitants. These Guests so disposed of, with their house of clay the Pipkin, place over a gentle fire, and by degrees warm them, till they being pleased with their habitation begin to simper, and dance a little; then do you promote their pa-

stime

time by stirring with a stick, (as in the last Chapter you were directed.) But if they finding the place too hot for them, should endeavour to escape by boiling over, which you'l soon discover by the rout and bustle, and rising of the water; release them, not from the Vessels but fix the Pipkin in a cooler place; yet so, that they may always dance, and boil leisurely. If you find that a little of this Liquor being pour'd on the ground, if cold, is willing by your fingers to be reduced to powder, you may conclude that the operation has succeeded well, and ought now to be concluded. Having stood long enough to loose its acquired heat, and will suffer you to handle it; part these fellow-sufferers, by taking the Venice-Turpentine into your wet hands, and therewith squeez from it its friend the water, as clean as possibly; roll it into the figure of a ball, and after a day or two pound and beat it into fine powder, and in a fit place set it to dry, but not too near the fire, which will melt it; and lastly, imprison it in a Gallipot.

This Operation is just like the former; but the two Turpentines are at variance, and differ in their colours; for this is as white as Paper, the other, in the last Chapter, as yellow as Amber: You must therefore of necessity judge this most excellent for the present use; although 'tis more often to be washt with it, before it will endure and acquire a glittering Polish.

Having advanced thus far, let us now proceed to compose the Varnish, by joining one ounce of this powder'd Turpentine to half a pint of Seed-Lace-varnish, in a bottle twice as large as the things you put in, close stopt. When it has stood some small time on an easie fire, take it off, unstop, and shake it: be sure to do so, until the Turpentine be dissolved to the bigness of a large Pea; and after two days have both cool'd and settled it, decant and separate the clearest, which is now in readiness for your work. Your ·piece therefore lying before you drawn and finished, waiting for security against all damages, fortifie after this manner. Take a neat, clean, varnish-Pencil, large or small, as your work is in its Area, surface and breadth; for a large Table or Box requires a great Pencil, and so the contrary. This Pencil being dipt into a Gallipot, wherein you have poured some of the said varnish; when you take it out, always stroke it against the sides of the pot, for fear it should be too full and overburthened with varnish, which will incur this inconvenience, That 'twill lie thick and rough in some places, whereas a smooth and even superficies is its greatest beauty. This, without any distinction, must wash over your whole work, both draught and ground: And you must do it five or six times, as you see the gold and metals keep their colour, gently warming and throughly drying it between every wash; and indeed it must be but just warm, for if more, 'twill ruine all your labour. Having observed these rules, as also that it must by all means be evenly and smoothly done; let it have rest for three or four days before you attempt

any

any thing further upon it. After this time is past, provide some Tripole, scraped with a piece of glass, and a fine rag, which dipt in a bason of water, and some powder of the same Tripole being lickt up by the said cloth, therewith in a moderate way, neither too hard or too soft, rub and stroke, until it becomes smooth and glossy; but if it should come so near your gold or draught as to molest and displace it, utterly desist, and rub no more there, but let your chief aim be to render your ground or black, bright and smooth, for there your wavings and unevenefs will be most discernable. Now to fetch of the Tripolee, take the softest Spunge soak'd in water, and with it wash it off, and a clean cloth or rag to dry and free it from all the Tripolee that remains. But because this will not free the crevises and fine lines from it, mingle a little oyl with a like quantity of Lamblack, and grease your Table all over with the same : now to fetch off this too, labour and rub with a fine cloath, until your Lamblack and Oyl vanish and disappear. To conclude this tedious business; Take one fine clean rag more, and therewith rub and stroak until a glofs is acquired, and that it glissen and reflect your face like a Mirror or Looking-glass.

I suppofe by this time it is apparent, what trouble, pains, care, and accuracy, accompany our Undertakings ; and if to these you prefix the Skill, Fancy, and fine Hand of the Artist ; I say all these must enhance, and set an high price upon good Japan-work.

These instructions for composing Varnishes, the must needful and best for all works of this kind, being thus fully laid down ; it will be no ways prejudicial to give some Rules, which must be most strictly observed in all sorts of Varnishing, and to inform you how you may employ these Varnishes about other Woods ; or to lay Blacks, and other colours, which are much in vogue with us and the Indians. We grant, it is not a part of Japan-work properly, but rather foreign to that design, but its univerfal benefit will abundantly compensate for that pretence, and the knowledge of it cannot certainly prove burthensome to any : But to those especially it is advantageous, who living in the Country remote from Artists, cannot without great trouble move or alter any thing they have by them, unlefs affisted by this our information.

CHAP. III.

General Rules to be diligently obferved in all manner of Varnishing.

I Am very follicitous that your Work should succeed, and therefore take all imaginable care to guide you, fo that you cannot possibly mifcarry ; and in order thereunto shall propose Rules and gene-

general Cautions,, which I defire you would have always in mind, and call them to your affiftance in all your undertakings.

1. Therefore let your wood which you intend to varnifh be clofe-grained, exempt and free from all knots and greafinefs, very fmooth, clean, and well rufh't.

2. Lay all your Colours and Blacks exquifitely even and fmooth; and where ever mole-hills and knobs, afperities and roughnefs in colours or varnifh offer to appear, with your Rufh fweep them off, and tell them their room is more acceptable to you than their company. If this ill ufage will not terrifie them, or make them avoid your work, give them no better entertainment than you did before, but maintain your former feverity, and with your Rufh whip them off, as often as they moleft you.

3. Keep your work always warm, by no means hot, which will certainly blifter or crack it; and if that mifchance through inadvertency fhould happen, tis next to irreparable, and nothing lefs than fcraping off all the varnifh can rectifie the mifcarriage.

4. Let your work be throughly dry, after every diftinct wafh; for neglect in this point introduces the fault again, of which we warned you in the fecond rule, That your varnifh fhould not be rough and knobby.

5. Let your work lie by and reft, as long as your convenience will admit, after tis varnifhed; for the better will your endeavours prove, the longer it ftands after this operation.

6. Be mindful to begin your varnifhing ftroak in the middle of the table or box that you have provided for that work, and not in full length from one end to the other, fo that your brufh being planted in the middle of your board, ftrike it to one end; then taking it off, fix it to the place you began at, and draw or extend it to the other end; fo muft you do till the whole plane or content be varnifhed over. We have reafons too for this caution, which if neglected, has feveral faults and prejudices attending it; for if you fhould undertake at one ftroak to move your Pencil from end to end, it would fo happen that you would overlap the edges and mouldings of your box; this overlapping is, when you fee the varnifh lie in drops and fplafhes, not laid by your brufh, but caufed by your brufhes being at the beginning of the ftroak overcharg'd and too full of varnifh, and therefore we advife you to ftroke your pencil once or twice againft the fides of the Gallipot, to obftruct and hinder this fuperfluity; fmall experience will difcover thefe miftakes.

7. When you come to polifh, let your Tripolee be fcraped with glafs or a knife: for fine work your rags muft be fine, and your Tripolee too delicately fmall, and powder-like; and fo for common work, coarfe linnen, and coarfer Tripolee will be very ferviceable: let your hand be moderately hard, but very even, in all your polifhing-ftroaks; and remember to polifh and brighten one place, as much as for that time you intend to do, before you forfake it, and pafs over to another.   For   8. Re-

8. Remember, never to polish your work as smooth as you intend at one time, but let it rest two or three days if you can after the first polishing, and then give it the finishing and concluding stroak. Be circumspect likewise that you come nor near the wood, to make your piece look thin, hungry, and threadbare: should you therefore injure your workmanship after this manner, it will demand another varnishing for satisfaction and reparation.

9. Take a large quantity of Tripolee at the first polishing, till it begins to become smooth; afterwards, a very small parcel will suffice. Circumspectly examin your Tripolee and clout, least some mischievous, unwelcom gravel, grittinefs, or grating part, unawares steal in, and rafe or scratch your work; it will prove no easie matter to hide the flaw and damage: and if ever it should so happen, you must retrieve your negligence by your labour, and with your cloath wrapt about your forefinger polish the faulty place until you have brought it to a good understanding and evenness with the rest of the piece, and the wounded part to be no more visible.

10. When you refolve to clear up your work, and put it in its best apparel, remove and wash off your Tripolee with a Spunge and water: drink up that water with dry linnen, and with oyl mixt with Lamblack anoint the whole face of your work; let no corner or moulding escape, for this will totally free your piece from the lurking Tripolee. Now tis time that these should withdraw, and as they turned out the Tripolee, fo must a clean linnen rag displace them, and put them to shift for new quarters; and then with another clean, very fine, foft, dry cloath, rub it all over; spare no place, or pains, but falute it all with a nimble, quick stroak, and as hard an hand, and the fruits of your industry will be a dazling luftre, and an incomparable glofs.

Laftly, for white-work, be kind and gentle to it, let your hand be light and even, and your skill in polishing it neat and curious; and observe, that when tis to be cleared up, you must not pollute and dawb it with Lamblack, but oblige it with oyl and fine flower instead thereof.

To conclude, let this Chapter be well studied, and remember, that without it you cannot regularly or safely perform the task: This is the Common-place-book, to which I shall continually refer you; and if you will prove negligent and remifs in this particular, I shall prophefie, that nothing can fo infallibly attend you as Error and Difappointment.

F CHAP.

CHAP. IV.

Of varnishing Woods *without* Colour.

To varnish Olive-wood.

WHat remains then, but that from Precept we proceed to Practice, that from mean and ordinary endeavours we successively rise to the excellence and perfection of this Art. To begin with Olive-wood, which for Tables, Stands, Cabinets, &c, has been highly in request amongst us; that which is cleanly workt off, void of flaws, cracks, and asperities, is a fit subject for our skill to be exercised in. Having rushed it all over diligently, set it by a weak fire, or some place where it may receive heat; and in this warm condition, wash it over ten or twelve times with Seed-Lace-varnish, that remained after you had poured off the top for a better use, with a pencil proportioned to the bigness of your Table or Stand, or the like; let it throughly dry between every wash; and if any roughness come in sight, rush 'em off as fast as you meet with them. After all this, welcom it with your Rush until tis smooth, and when very dry, anoint it six several times with the top or finest part of the aforesaid Seed-Lace-varnish. After three days standing call for Tripolee scraped with a knife; and with a cloth, dipt first in water, then in powdered Tripolee, polish and rub it till it acquire a smoothness and gloss: but be circumspect and shie of rubbing too much, which will fret and wear off the varnish, that cannot easily be repair'd: If when you have labour'd for some time, you use the rag often wetted, without Tripolee, you will obtain the better gloss. Then wipe of your Tripolee with a spunge full of water, the water with a dry rag; grease it with Lamblack and Oyl all over; wipe off that with a cloth, and clear it up with another, as I have most fully shewed in the last Chapter, to which I refer you. If after all this pains your work look dull, and your varnish misty, which polishing before tis dry, and damp weather will effect; give it a slight polish, clear it up, and that will restore its pristine beauty: If you have been too niggardly of your varnish, and there is not enough to bear and endure a polish, use again your finest Seed-Lace, and afford it four or five washes more; after two days quietness polish and clear it up. Should any one desire to keep the true natural, and genuine colour of the wood, I council him to employ the white-varnish formerly mentioned, as every where answerable to his purpose; for this being of a reddish tawny colour, and so often washed with it, must necessarily heighten and increase the natural one of the Olive.

To varnish Walnut-wood.

To avoid a tedious and troublesom repetition or tautology, I shall refer you to the last Chapter, and desire you to observe the
same

same method exactly for varnishing Walnut, that I give you for Olive. And farther take notice, that those Rules will hold good also for all forts of wood, that are of a clofe, fmooth grain, fuch are Yew, Box, the Lime-tree, and Pear-tree, &c. Thus much may fuffice for varnifhing woods without colour; we pafs over from hence to treat of the adorning woods with colour, and of each in its order.

CHAP. V.

Of varnishing WOODS *with Colour.*

Of Black Varnishing or Japan.

BLack varnifhing is done in imitation of Japan-work: and becaufe the making this very good is a great ornament to the whole undertaking, I fhall give you the beft account I can poffibly for the making it. Having provided wood, clofe-grained, and well wrought off, rufh it fmooth, and keep it warm by a fire, or in fome hot place; but be always cautious, that whilft you varnifh, you fuffer not the piece to take the eye of the fire, that is, come fo near it as to burn, fcorch, or blifter your work, which is an unpardonable fault, and remedied no other way when committed but by fcraping off the varnifh, as I hinted in the Chapter of Rules and Directions. Thofe that make it their trade, generally work in a Stove, which is beyond all difpute the beft and fafeft way; and I would advife thofe, who intend to make it their imployment, to ufe no other; becaufe it gives an even and moderate heat to all parts of the room: but thofe who for pleafure, fancy, and diverfion only, practife; for them I fay, a great fire in a clofe, warm chamber, may perform it as well. In the next place, pour fome of the thickeft Seed-Lace-varnifh into a Gallipot, adding to it as much Lamblack as will at the firft wafh blacken and difcolour the work; the Colour-fhops furnifh you with it for 2d, 4d, or 6d the barrel, whofe price is equal to its bignefs: With this varnifh and black mixt together varnifh over your thing three times, permitting it to dry throughly between every turn. After this, take more of the Lac-varnifh, and mix with it Lampblack to the fame degree of thicknefs with the former. This is the only black for this bufinefs, I prefer it before Ivory, (tho fome differ with me on this point;) this is a fine, foft, and a very deep black, and agrees beft with the varnifh; how you fhall make it, I will in the next Section direct you. With this black compofition wafh it over three times, between each of them rufhing it fmooth, and fuffering it cleaverly to dry. Then with a quarter of a pint of the thickeft Seed-Lace, mix of Venice Turpentine the bignefs of a walnut, and fhake them together until it is diffolved, and obferve this proportion in lefs or greater quantities. Now put in Lamp-black enough to colour it,

and

and no more, and with this wash it fix times, letting it stand 12
hours between the three first and the three last washings. Having
thus cloathed the piece with ordinary varnish as with a common
under-garment, we now intend to put on its gayest apparrel, and
cover it all over with the top and finest of the Seed-Lac-varnish,
which must also be just coloured and tinged with the Lamp-black:
twelve times must it be varnished with this, standing as many
hours between the six first and the six last washings, with this never to be forgotten caution, That they stand till they are dried between every distinct varnishing. After all this give it rest for five
or six days before you attempt to polish it; that time being expired, take water and Tripolee, and polish it according to the directions I have assigned and taught you in the Chapter for Olive-
wood: but however take along with you this further remark,
That you allow three times distinct from each other for polishing;
for the first, labour at it till tis almost smooth, and let it stand still
two days; the next time, polish till it is very near enough and sufficient: lay it aside then for five or six days; after which, lastly,
polish off, and clear it up as you were before instructed. Following this course, I have, I will assure you, made as good, as glossy,
and beautiful a Black, as ever was wrought by an English hand,
and to all appearance it was no way inferior to the Indian.

I promised to detect and lay open the whole Art, and do resolve
by no means to fall short of my engagement. I intend therefore
to pleasure you with another way to make good Black, and having
variety you may take your choice, and try either, as your fancy
or Genius is inclined. I must confess, I have made excellent good
black this way too, and such as in all respects would match and
parallel the foregoing. Lay your blacks as before, and take of the
best Seed-Lac-varnish, and the White-varnish, (I mean the first
White that I taught you to make in this Book) an equal quantity,
and vouchsafe to give it a tincture only of your Lamp or Ivory-
black; wash your work with it six or eight times, let it stand the
space of a day or two, and dry between every turn; then repeat it
four or five times more, keeping it but just warm, and having rest-
ed a day or so, anoint it as often with the fine Seed-Lac-varnish only. To conclude, in a weeks time, after all this has been done, it
will be dry enough to polish, and not before, which you may then
do, and clear it up. You will observe, that your glossy performances after some little time may happen to wax dull, misty, and
heavy; which a slight polish will remedy, with clearing it up afterward. Now the causes of this disappointment are two; either
first, your varnish is not reasonably well dried, or it has not a sufficient body of varnish; both these occasion it to mist, and, as it
were, to purl. Tis no hard task to distinguish them: if the former is in fault, it will appear dull, but of a full body, and smooth;
if the latter, the work will look hungry, and so bare, that you may
almost, if not quite, see the very grain of the wood through your
                                                              varnish

varnish. This last fault is mended by five or six washes more of your fine Seed-Lace; the other is assisted by frequent polishings, with discretion. One Memorandum I had almost passed over in silence, which I presume I have not any where mentioned; You must look upon it as a necessary remark, and by no means to be omitted, and this it is; To be industriously careful, in laying on your colours and varnish, never to strike your pencil twice over the same place, for it will make your varnish or colours lie rough and ugly: but let every stroak anoint a place not washt before, carrying a steady, quick, and even hand; beginning at the middle of the table, and so conveying your brush to either end, until the whole surface has been passed over. Perhaps I have here spoken the same thing over and over again; in justification whereof, I alledge what Seneca did to those, who objected that he was guilty of tautologie, and repetition; " I only (says he) inculcate often the " same precepts to those who commit and react the same vices: This is my case; if you charge me with that fault, my plea is his; I often admonish you, and insert many cautions which refer to the same error, and apply 'em to those who are subject to frequent miscarriages.

To make Lamp-black.

Being furnished with a Lamp that has three or four Spouts, for as many lights and cotton-week, which you may have at the Tallow-chandlers, twisted up so big that it will but just go into the nose of your Spouts; for the greater light they make, the larger quantity of black is afforded. Procure a quart of oyl, by the Oyl-shops rated at 6d. and so much will make black enough to use about a large Cabinet. Get a thing to receive your black in, such in shape and substance as you may often see is planted over a candle to keep the flame and smoak from the roof or ceiling of a room. Having placed your weecks in their proper apartment, and put in the oyl, fire or light 'em, and fix your receiver over them so close, that the flame may almost touch them. After it has continued so the space of half an hour, take off your receiver, and with a feather strike and sweep off all the black on it. Snuff your weecks, and put it on again, but forget not to supply your Lamp with oyl, as often as occasion shall require; and when you imagine more black is stuck to the receiver, do as before directed: and thus continue and persevere, until you have obtained black enough, or that all your oyl is burnt up and exhausted. This is that which is properly called Lamp-black, and is of excellent use for black varnish.

White Varnishing or Japan.

You cannot be over-nice and curious in making white Japan; nothing must be used that will either foil or pollute it, in laying on the colour, or in varnishing. Your first necessary therefore is Isinglass-size, (to make which the next Section shall instruct you;)

G scrape

scrape into it as much whiting, as will make it of a reasonable
thickness and consistence; or so long, till by a stroak with your
pencil dipt into it, it will whiten the body which your brush has
passed over; your own discretion is the best guide. Suffer it not
to be in extreams, either too thick or too thin; but with your
brush, made of the softest Hogs-hair, mix and incorporate very
well the whiting with your size. This being prepared, whiten
your work once over with it, and having stood till tis throughly
dry, do it all over again; and when dry, repeat it a third time:
after which let it stand twelve hours, but be sure to cover and de-
fend it from dust before tis varnish't. Take then some rushes;
rush it as smooth and as close to the wood as you can conveniently.
This done, procure some white flake, with which the Colour-shops
can furnish you; mix it too with your size only, that it may lie
with a full, fair body on your piece. With this, three several
times whiten your work, giving it sufficient time to dry between
each of them; then rush it extraordinarily smooth, but be not
now so bold as you were before; adventure not to come near the
wood, but by all means keep your distance. These two sorts of
white being used, we charge you with a third, and that is, white
Starch, boiled in fair water, until it come to be somewhat thick,
and with it almost blood-warm wash over the whole, twice; never
forgetting that it should dry between every turn. After 24 hours
rest, take the finest of your white-varnish, and with a pencil (first
washed in spirit to clean it from dust) anoint or varnish your work
six or seven times, and after a day or two do the like again. These
two fits of varnishing, if done with a fine careful hand, will give it
a better gloss than if it were polish't; if not so accurately performed, tis requisite to polish it; and in order thereunto, you must bestow five or six washes of varnishing more than to the former : so
that if tis done so well, that it stands not in need of a polish, two
turns of varnishing will suffice; but if it must be polish't, three are
absolutely required, besides a weeks rest before you begin polishing. Care and neatness should attend this operation from one end
to the other; for in polishing, your Linnen and Tripolee must be
both of the finest; your hand light and gentle, your cloth neither
too wet, or too dry; and when you clear it up, and give it the finishing, concluding stroak, fine flower and oyl must be admitted to
the performance, but Lamp-black utterly laid aside and excluded.

To make Isinglass-Size.

Take an ounce of Isinglass, divided or broke into small pieces;
let it stand in a clean Pipkin, accompanied with a pint and a half of
fair water, for twelve hours together   Place the vessel in a gentle fire, suffer it to boil mighty leisurely, and continue smiling and
simpering, till it is wholly consumed and dissolved in the water.
After the water it self is wasted and boiled away to a pint or less,
remove it, and let it stand in a convenient place to cool. This when
cold,

cold will turn to a Jelly, which we call Ifinglafs-fize. You are
advifed to make no more than what will ferve your prefent occafions, for two or three days will totally deprive it of its ftrength
and virtue. 'Tis of great ufe, not only in the foregoing white-varnifh, but feveral other things, hereafter to be mentioned.

To make Blew-Japan.

This task calls for feveral ingredients, and thofe too diverfly
prepared, before they can be admitted to the compofition. In the
front white-lead appears, which muft be ground with Gum-water
very finely on a Marble-ftone. The next in rank is fome of the
beft and fineft Smalt, (to be met with in the Colour-fhops,) which
you muft mix with Ifinglafs-fize ; adding, of your white-lead fo
grinded, a quantity proportionable to the Blew you intermix
with 'em, or as you would have it be in ftrength of body. All thefe
well ftirred and temper'd together, being arrived to the confiftence
and thicknefs of common Paint, wafh over your work with it,
and, when perfectly dry, do the like three or four times, until you
obferve your Blew lies with a good fair body ; if it fhould fo fall
out, that the Blew fhould be too pale and weak, put more Smalt,
and no white-lead into your fize. Having rufh't it very
fmooth, ftrike it over again with this ftronger Blew : foon after,
yet not till it is very dry, with a clean pencil give it, at two feveral times, as many wafhings with the cleareft Ifinglafs-fize alone ;
and lay it afide for two days carefully covered, to preferve it from
duft: The fame diligence forget not in making White-Japan,
which does as abfolutely require a covering, until either of them
is fecured by a proper mantle of their own, varnifh, which is fufficient to guard 'em againft all injuries of duft or dirt. But to proceed : When you have warmed it by the fire, imploy again your
cleaneft pencil, dipt in a fmall portion of white-varnifh , anointing
your work feven or eight times ; defift then for one day or two,
after which wafh it again as often as before. Lay it afide for the
fame fpace of time, which being expired, repeat your wafhes the
third and laft time, as often as formerly. So many operations
certainly deferve fome leifure minuts, and a week at leaft muft be
pafs'd over, before you dare prefume to polifh it. When that is
done, with Lamblack and oyl clear it up, and lend it a gliftening,
fmooth, and pleafant countenance. Obferve, that your Blews being more deep and dark, thin or pale, depends wholly upon the
different quantities of white-lead, that are mixt with the Smalt after the firft wafhes : for as a fmall proportion of Lead introduces
the firft, fo a greater plenty occafions the latter.

Let this ferve for a general caution in laying either Blews,
White, or any other colours with Ifinglafs-fize ; Let it not be
too ftrong, but rather on the contrary very weak, but juft fufficient to bind your colours, or make them ftick on your work : for if
it be otherwife, it will be apt to crack and flie off. But laft of all,
when

when you lay or wash with clear Isinglass, to keep you varnish from soaking into, or tarnishing your colours, then let it be of a strong and full body.

To make Gum-water

Hardly any can be ignorant of the making of this; 'tis very common, and easie, and the composition consists of two bodies only. In three quarters of a pint of fair water dissolve one ounce of the whitest Gum-Arabick, carefully and cleanly picked: If you keep stirring and shaking it, the sooner 'twill be dissolved; which done, strain it through a fine Holland-rag into a bottle, and if you want it, use it.

To make Red-Japan.

This beautiful colour is made several ways, and we want not drugs and mixtures to vary the different Reds, and humour all fancies whatsoever. I shall confine their variety to three heads: 1. The common usual Red; 2. the deep, dark; and lastly, the light, pale Red. Of these in their order.

In contriving the first, Vermilion deservedly claims the chief place: 'Tis mixt with common size by some, by others with the thickest of Seed-Lace. The last I judge most fit and useful, for this reason; because it will not then break off in polishing, as that mixt with size frequently does: neither is it more chargeable, seeing it helps better to bear the body of varnish that shall be spread over it; Your mixture should keep a medium between thick and thin; 'tis difficult, and almost impossible to assign exact Rules for mingling your Colours, in general we tell you between both extremes; small practice and experience will master this seeming difficulty. Your work being ready and warm, produce your Vermilion well mixt with the varnish, and salute it four times with it; then allow it time to dry, and if your Reds be full, and in a good body to your liking, rush it very smooth: so done, wash it eight times with the ordinary Seed-Lac-varnish, and grant it a repose for twelve hours; then rush it again, though slightly, to make it look smooth. And lastly, for a fine outward covering bestow eight or ten washes of your best Seed-Lace-varnish upon it: and having laid it by for five or six days bring it forth to polish, and clear it up with Oyl and Lamblack.

The next in succession to be discours'd on is the dark, deep Red. When you have laid on your common Red as before directed, take Dragons-blood, reduce it to a very small dust or powder, and as your judgment and fancy are inclined, mix it, a little at a time, with your varnish; and indeed you will find, that a very small portion will extreamly heighten your colour, as also that every wash will render it deeper; but when you find it has acquired a colour almost as deep as you design, forbear, for you must remember you have more varnish of Seed-Lace to lay on, which will add and supply what is wanting. Consider therefore how many washes

are

are ftill to be laid, and according to that ufe your Sanguis Draconis, or Dragons-blood. This performance differs no way from the former, but muft be managed by thofe rules given for polifhing and clearing the other Red, the Sanguis only excepted.

But in the third place, to oblige any perfon that is an admirer of a pale Red, we affign thefe inftruations. Take white-lead finely ground with your Muller on the Marble-ftone, you muft grind it dry; mix it with your vermilion till it becomes paler than you would have it, for the varnifh will heighten it : ftir therefore vermilion, white-lead, and varnifh together very briskly; which done, give your work four wafhes, and then follow clofely the preferiptions laid down for the firft Red varnifh. You muft in the foregoing mixture confult with your felf, how many times you are to varnifh after the Red is laid; for if many, confider how they will increafe and heighten the colour, which for that reafon muft be paler, and have a more large portion of white-lead allotted it. By thefe means we have opened a fpatious field, we have difcovered the very nature of the thing; our Art has been freely difplayed,and we have been neither penurious or niggardly in our communications : What admirable Produats may we expeat, when a lively and unlimited fancie is exercifed in an Art that is equally boundlefs and unconfined.

To lay or make Chefnut-colour-Japan.

This colour is now very much ufed, and of great efteem, efpecially for Coaches; I have alfo made other things, as Tables, Stands, and Looking-glafs-frames. I muft of neceffity declare, that it fets off Gold and Metals well : and becaufe variety in every thing that is new is acceptable, but chiefly to the ingenious Gentry, for whom thefe pages are intended, I could not in filence pafs this colour over.

The things that make up this colour are Indian Red, or elfe Brown red Oaker, which will ferve as well : of either, what quantity you imagin will ferve your turn, and with a Muller or Marble-ftone grind it, mixed with ordinary fize, as fine as butter. From thence tranflate it to a pottinger; then take a little white-lead, and laborioufly grind it after the former manner, and with the fame fize : In the third place, have Lamblack ready by you ; mix this and the white-lead with the Indian Red or Oaker in the pottinger, ftirring and incorporating them together. If the colour produced by thefe three be too bright, darken it with Lamblack ; if too dark and fad, affift it with white-lead ; this do, until you have maftered the colour you wifh for. One thing here commands your memory and obfervation; The fame colour exaatly which you make when tis thus mixt and wet, will alfo arife when tis varnifhed, although when tis laid and dry, twill look otherwife. Now when the colours are thus managed in the pottinger, fet it over a gentle fire, put to it fo much common fize as will give it a fit temper to work, (neither too thick, or too thin.) Being thus qualified for

bufibusinels, call for a fine proportionable Hogs-hair brush, with it wash over smoothly your piece ; let it dry, and repeat until your colour lie full and fair.   Again, give it a drying time, and rush it smooth, but by no means close to the wood, unless you intend to begin your work anew, and varnish it a second time.   After a days rest, adorn it with three or four washes of the fine Seed-Lace-varnish ; when that is also dried on, varnish it up to a body, fit to receive a polish, with your white varnish.   To conclude, its due and necessary time being spent, polish and clear it up with Lamblack and Oyl.

To make an Olive-colour.

This performance is every way answerable to the former ; only instead of those put English Pinck : grind it with common size, and when it has attained the consistence of butter, convey it to a pottinger, and there Lamblack and White-lead mixt with it produce the Olive-colour ; if too light, Lamblack will prevent it, if too dark the other.   But farther, if you think it looks too green, take raw Umber, grinded very fine with size ; add of that enough to take away that greenefs : And nothing then remains but a due heed and obfervance of the foregoing rules for Chefnut.   But before we leave this Section, remember, That all colours laid in size will not endure so violent a polish as those in varnish, but are more subject to be rubb'd off.

By these methods you may make any colour you can fancie ; with this admonition, That all colours, which are light and apt to tarnish, and loose their glofly beauty with Seed-Lace, must be humour'd and varnished with White-varnish, the Seed-Lace being prejudicial.

CHAP. VI.

To work Metals or Colours with Gum-water.

WHenfoever you defign to work Japan in Gum-water, you are advifed to mix all your Metals and Colours, and every thing you make ufe of, with this Gum-water.   But becaufe there is no general Rule without exception ; therefore we underftand all colours, except thofe which before we called Tranfparent ones, for they require a different and diftinct way of operation, as the beginning of this Treatife has directed.

When you defign a mixture, forget not to ftir the ingredients very well, together with the water, in a Mufcle-fhell, which I conceive is more proper for this undertaking, and for that reafon defired you to furnifh your felf with a great number of them.   Be cautious, I befeech you, that you make not the mixture of your metals or colours with the gum-water either too thick or thin, but endeavour to keep the golden mean between both, that it may run

fine

fine and smoothly from your pencil. Beside, be not prodigal, lavish, and profuse of your metals, but make a quantity requisite for your present business only, and provide not for time to come ; for from a mixture of this nature, made in too large a proportion, several inconveniences arise. As first, in some short time, the metals standing useless, wax dry, so that they must be wetted for a second emploiment with the said gum-water, which by repetition corrupts both the metal and the colour, by receiving too much of gum in them : and although this might be likewise prevented, by adding fair water instead of that mixt with gum ; yet in spite of all care and diligence, and beyond expectation too, another trouble and fault accompanies it, and that is, the dust will gather to them and render 'em unfit and unserviceable. Again, for your colours especially, your Shells must be often shifted and changed, otherwise the gum and colours will be both knobby and drie, in that unseemly posture sticking to your shells. I believe it will be your own negligence, and the fault will lie at your door, if after every minute caution and remark, whereby you may not fail of success if they are observed, you should through inadvertency miscarry. But to proceed : Your metals or colours thus prepared, well mixed, and ready for the business, stir them with the pencil about the shell, and draw it often on the side of the shell, that it may not be overloaded with the metal, when you design to draw small stroaks ; on the other side, not too drie, because you must be careful in making all your stroaks full and fair, by no means thin and craggy ; carry your hand even and steddy, and finish your line before you draw off your hand, otherwise you may incur making the stroak uneven, and bigger in one place than another. But when you attempt great broad things, as Leaves, or large work, then charge your pencil very full, with this proviso only that it does not drop. Here is one observation to be made for Gum-water, which in Gold-size is useless and unnecessary, and indeed very advantagious for learners, and the unskilful especially, and by them in a particular manner to be remarkt and observed. But first, tis useful for all ; for that place you intend to make your draught in must be rubbed with a Tripolee-cloth : the reason is this ; your black, when cleared up, will be so glossy, and as it were greasie, that your metal or colour will not lie on it, unless it be primed with the Tripolee in that manner. So when you find any such greasiness on your work, rub it with your Tripolee-cloth, and permit it to dry ; after which you will perceive the draught of your pencil to be smooth and neat, and to your liking and satisfaction.

Now that which I before spake of in behalf of beginners is this : It may very reasonably be supposed, that a practitioner in his first attempts may not frame his piece even and regular, or his lines at a due distance : now upon these or any other accounts, if he is displeased at his own handy-work, he may with this useful Tripolee-cloth wipe out all, or any part which he thinks unworthy to stand,

and

and on the fame fpot erect a new draught; by thefe means he may
mend, add, blot out, and alter, until the whole fabrick be of one
entire make, good and anfwerable to each part of the undertaking.
I cannot better in words exprefs my felf, or with my Pen deliver
more full or plain rules for mixing your colours and metals; neither can I with my tongue more fteadily guide your hand and pencil.   I am apt to flatter my felf fo far, as to believe what I have
communicated may abundantly fuffice, and fhall therefore add nothing more with relation to laying metals or colours, and the manner or method of working them in Gum-water.   That part of our
Profeffion which we call Setting off, or, which is the fame thing
in other words, Seeding of Flowers, Veining of Leaves, Drawing of Faces, and making Garments, defires not our prefent con-
fideration, but fhall be handled in the following pages.

CHAP. VII.

To make Gold-fize.

THis is the other famous compofition, which is in great efteem
and ufe for laying metals and colours, and ought in due manner to be made known; but we fhall firft give you the method of
mixing thofe things which are concerned in its production.   Their
names and quantities are, of Gum animæ one ounce, Gum Efpal-
tum one ounce, Lethergi of Gold half an ounce; Red-lead, brown
Umber, of each the like portion.   To thefe, fhut altogether in a
new earthen pipkin, large enough to hold one third more than you
put in, pour of Linfeed oyl a quarter of a pint, of drying oyl half
a pint, with which you may be furnifhed at the colour-fhops.
Place this earthen veffel thus loaded over a gentle fire, that does
not flame in the leaft, keeping it continually fo warm, that it may
but juft bubble up, or almoft boil; fhould it rife over, your chimny and materials would be in danger: if you perceive it fwelling,
and endeavouring to pafs its bounds, remove it from that hot place
to a more cool and gentle.   When firft it begins to fimper and boil
a little, with a ftick keep moving and ftirring it, until the whole
mafs of Gums be incorporated and melted; not that you muft defift or forbear ftirring until it become as thick and ropy as Treacle,
for then it is fufficiently boiled.   This done, convey the pipkin to
a cool place, and there let it reft, till the extremity of heat is over.
After which time, ftrain it through a coarfe linnen cloth into another earthen pot, there to cool, and lie ready for ufe.
   This is the manner of its compofition.   I fhall now infert the
ways of working it.   When your bufinefs fhall call for this Size,
bring forth what quantity you require for the prefent, and put it
into a mufcle-fhell with as much oyl of Turpentine as will diffolve
the fize, and make it as thin as the bottom of your Seed-Lacc.

Hold

Hold it over a candle, and, when melted, strain it through a Linnen rag into another shell. To both these add vermilion enough to make it of a darkish red; but if this make it too thick for drawing, afford it as much oyl of Turpentine as will make it thin enough for that purpose. The main, and indeed only design of this Size, is for laying on of Metals, which after this manner must be performed.

When you have wrought your work, and that which you intend to decipher on it; draw this Size all over that part, and that part only, which you resolve shall be guilded or adorned with gold, paffing over those places where you think to lay your other metal or colours, as Copper, Silver, or the like. Your Size being thus wrought for the Gold, let it stand till tis so dry, that when you put your finger upon any of it, it may be glutinous and clammy, and stick a little, but not so moist that the least spot or speck should come off with your fingers, not unlike to thick glue when tis half dry. When you find it agrees with the characters we have given you, conclude that to be the critical minute, the very nick of time, wherein you must apply your Gold; then take a piece of soft, washt leather, or the like: this being wrapt about your forefinger, dip it into your gold-dust, and rub where the gold-size is laid, for it will stick on the size, and no where else. If any dust of Gold l'es scattered about your work, with a fine varnishing-brush, that hath not been used, brush or wipe it all into your gold-paper. This being thus finished, take your pencil in hand again; draw that part which you design for Copper with Gold-size also; and when dry, cover it with Copper after the same method that you received for Gold. A third time weild your instrument, the pencil, and lay Size for Silver, and operate as aforesaid; so likewise for all dead metals, wheresoever you design them: Only take this remark along with you, That you lay your metals succeffively one after another, suffering each to dry and be covered, before you begin a diftinct one; as for instance, Your Gold-size must be dry, and guilded before you proceed farther, and so of the rest. After all these, lay your colours with gum-water if you are pleased to infert any, referving the Rocks for the last labour; which how to perform, in the succeeding discourse shall be demonstrated.

It may often so fall out, that you'l mix more Gold-size than at one time may be confumed, or you may be called off from your bufinefs for a day or more. Now to preserve it entire and moist enough, and in condition fit to work against next time, obferve that after it has stood five or six hours, a film or skin will arise and overfpread the furface of it: then put it in water, and let it remain there with the pencils covered too, until your next operation shall defire their affiftance; before which, you must stir it well together, and employ it as you think fit. If it should chance to grow thick, the old remedy, Venice Turpentine, will relieve it. But farther, if by frequent mixture with Turpentine, often putting into water, or

I   long

long standing, it becomes skinny, thick, and knobby, and by consequence unserviceable; the best use you can possibly put it to, is to cast it away.

I shall conclude this Chapter with my requests to you, so to order and compose your Size, that, being of a good mediocrity, neither too thick or thin, it may run smooth and clear, and your stroaks be fine and even; in some time you will be so skilful, and so delighted with your draught, that the most subtle, neat, and hairy lines will adorn your piece, and your work in all good qualities may, though not exceed, yet vie with, and parallel the Indian.

CHAP. VIII.

To varnish Prints with White Varnish.

PRocure a Board very fit and exact to the Print you resolve to varnish, and thus manage it. Get common Size, which you may have at the Colour-grocers; warming it by the fire, scraping whiting into it; make it of an indifferent thickness, and with the softest hogs-hair-brush, proportionable to your board, wash it once over, permitting it to dry: then white it again, and so repeat, till it lies with a fair body, and quite covers the grain of the wood, which may be of Deal, Oak, or any other. This done, take off your whiting with rushes very close, and smooth, but not so far as to discover the grain: then with flower and water make a paste thick as starch, and with your hand or brush work or dawb over the backside of your Print, with an even steddy hand lay your Print on the board, and stick it on as close as you can with all imaginable diligence. Suffer it not to cockle, wrinkle, or rise up in little bladders; if it should, press it down with your hand, but be sure your hands be extraordinarily clean and free from all dust, filth, and pollution when you come to paste on the Print, that it may not in the least be soiled, before tis varnished. Smooth down the whole paper with your hand, pass it over and over, that every part thereof may stick close and adhere to the whiting. I cannot here burden you with too many cautions and caveats; for if any the least part of your Print rise or bubble, the whole beauty and pride of the Picture is destroyed when you come to varnish. Being thus closely and carefully fixt to the board, set it by for 24. hours, or longer; then take the cleanest of your Isinglass-size, and with a soft pencil wash over your Print; but be certain it be dry before you pass it over again, which you must do with a quick hand, and not twice in a place; give it leisure to dry, and afford it one wash more, with two days rest: Afterwards with the finest and clearest of your white-varnish grant it six washes by a gentle heat, not too nigh the fire, to avoid blistering. When 24 hours

are

are past, give it eight washes with the said clear varnish : lay it a-side for two days, and then vouchsafe to anoint it six or seven times more, giving it leave to rest two or three days. Having advanced thus far, with linnen and Tripolee, both very fine, polish it, but with gentle and easie stroaks. Lastly, clear it up with oyl and flower.

This I must needs commend for a pleasing and ingenuous contrivance ; a new sort of Speculum or Lookingglass, which without deceit gives a double representation. Here the Prince and Subject may (and not irreverently) meet face to face ; here I may approach my King without the introduction of a Courtier : nay, tis so surprizing, that though I expect no shadow but that of my friend graven on the paper, it will in spite of me, in an instant too, draw my own Picture , so to the life, that you might without perjury swear tis the Original.   Amorous piece ! That (without the assistance of a Cunning man) obliges me with a survey of my Self and Mistress together ; and by this close conjunction, by these seeming caresses of her in Effigie , I counterfeit, nay almost antedate our more substantial enjoyments !   Kind Picture too ! which will permit me to gaze and admire without intermission, and can survey me as I do her, without anger or a blush !   I know very well no Apelles dare pretend to delineate or make an artificial beauty, that shall equal her natural : Know, that the perfections of her Body as far surpass the skill of the Pencil, as those of her Mind transcend the expressions and abilities of the Pen.   But yet, in one circumstance, and one only, the Picture does excel my Mistress ; the shadow is more lasting than the substance ; She will frown, wrinkles and old Age must overtake her ; but here she lives always Young, for ever blooming ; Clouds and Tempests are banish't from this Hemisphere, and she blesses me with a gracious and perpetual Smile.

CHAP. IX.

How to lay Speckles or Strewings on the out, or inside of Boxes, Drawers, Mouldings, &c.

HAving in readiness a quantity of Speckles, which you think may answer your present occasion, mix them with so much of your ordinary Lac-varnish, as will, being put both into a Gallipot, render them fit to work with a suitable Pencil , but by no means so thick as you would Colours. For this use only you must reserve a Brush, with which you must stir 'em very well, and your work being gently warmed by the fire, wash it over with it, and when dry, again.   This repeat, until your Speckles lie as thick and even, as you could wish or desire them ; afterwards beautifie them

I 2   with

with three or four washes of your Varnish mixt with Turpentine,
and you have concluded all, unless you intend to polish; for then,
having done every thing as above directed, tis required that you
give it eight or ten washings of your best Lac-varnish, which being all successively dried on, you are at liberty to polish it. All
sorts and variety of coloured Speckles may be thus ordered, except
Silver, the laying on of which choice metal deserves the best and
finest of your Seed-Lace, instead of the ordinary; and the best
white-varnish too, must be emploied to bring it to a polish; but if
you conclude upon not polishing it, be more sparing of your varnish, for fewer washes will suffice.

CHAP. X.

To lay Speckles on the drawing part of Japan-work, as Rocks, Garments, Flowers, &c.

BEfore you can proceed to try this experiment, a little Sieve must
be framed after this manner. Take a small box, such as Apo-
thecaries employ for Pills, something larger in compass than a
Crown-piece, about half an inch deep: strike out the bottom, and
in its place bind very strait about it fine Tiffanie, and to prevent
coming off fasten it on the outside of your box with thread, and reserve it for your necessities.

Now when your work expects to be adorned with Rocks, Flowers, or the like, use first your Pencil to varnish those places with,
and whilst it is wet put some of your strewings into the Sieve, and
gently shake it over the place designed for your Rock, until it appears answerable in Speckles to what you intended; but especially
when for Rocks, call for a pencil about the bigness of your finger,
one that is drie and new, and with it sweep all those stragling Speckles, that lie beyond the wet or varnished part, into the sides and
top of the Rock that is thus moistned; for there it will not only
stick, but render your work, thicker of Speckles in those places,
more beautiful, and oblige it with a kind of shadow and reflection.

This work admits of no idle hours, no interludes and vacations,
for as soon as one part is compleated, the other desires to undergo
the skill and contrivance of the Artist. When this Rock is drie,
the next must succeed in operation; and by this way of working
the one, when, and not before, the other is perfectly drie, you may,
like the Giants of old fighting against Jupiter, cast mountain upon
mountain, lay one rock upon or beside another, of different colours,
and as many shapes, until the whole enterprise of Rock-work is
completed. But observe, that in sweeping your Speckles into the
edges of each Rock, you intermix not one portion of scattered

parts

parts into a Rock of a different colour; let them therefore enjoy their proper ftrewings. When you thus lay your Rocks on your work being cold, it will certainly for the prefent look dull and hea-vy, nay to that degree, that you might very well fuggeft to your felf nothing lefs than the damage and ruine of the whole undertak-ing. But though no figns of life, beauty, or fhadow do appear, let not this ftartle or difcourage you; for when you have fecured it, as we directed before, this fright vanifhes, the dangerous Mormo or Bugbear difappears, its expected qualities fuddenly arife, and by the affiftance of your Securing-varnifh, it is decked with gay and beautiful apparrel.

CHAP. XI.

To make raifed work in imitation of Japan, and of the Pafte.

TO attempt the compofition of this Pafte, you muft provide a ftrong Gum-Arabick-water, charged with a double quantity of Gum to that we before taught you. Have in readinefs an ounce of Whiting, and a quarter of an ounce of the fineft and beft Bole-Armoniack; break them on your Grinding-ftone with the Gum-water, until they are made as fine as butter, but fo thin, that when moved into a Gallipot, it may but juft drop from the ftick with which you work and ftir it. If its condition be too thick, gum-water will relieve it; if too thin, you muft give it an addition of Whiting and Bole-Armoniack, as much as will make it capable of working well, and regularly The ftick that I fpake of before fhould refemble that of a Pencil-ftick, but it muft have a mere fharp and taper end. This dipt into your pafte, drop on the Rock, Tree, Flower, or Houfe which you purpofe to raife, and by repe-tition proceeding until tis raifed as high and even as you think con-venient. Prevent all bladdering in the pafte, which fcurvie fault proceeds from a carelefs and infufficient grinding and ftirring of the Whiting and Bole: fhould you with thefe blemifhes endeavour to raife, your work when dried will be full of holes, and thereby de-ftroy the beautie of it. The only way to prevent it in fome mea-fure, when fo dried, is, with a wet fine cloth wrapt about the fin-ger, to rub it over again and again, until the holes and cracks are quite choak't and ftopt up, and after its time of drying is expired, with a rufh and all imaginable induftry and care fmooth it.

Thefe affiftances I have laid down only in cafe of neceffity, by way of corrections for accidental mifcarriages; for your work will look abundantly neater, if thefe Errata are prevented by a Pafte in the beginning, well grinded and tempered before tis dropped on your work. You are defired farther to obferve, that in the Japan

K

raised-work for Garments, Rocks, &c. one part is elevated and
higher than the other; as in flowers, those that are first and nearest to the eye are highest, some leaves too that lie first are higher
than those that lie behind 'em : So in the pleats and foldings of
garments, those which seem to lie underneath, are always at the
greater distance. I will instance in but one more, and that is of
Rocks, where in position the first must always surmount and swell
beyond that which skulks behind, and is more remote : The rule
holds good in all things of a like nature, and if you endeavour to
counterfeit the Indians who take these measures, 'tis reasonable and
necessary to follow their prescriptions. I shall assign two ways for
its accomplishment, which, if truly and carefully copied out, will
come very near the Japan original.

Firſt, after your deſign is rais'd to a due height, whether Figure
or Flower, and well dried, with a little Gum-water, Vermilion, and
a Pencil, trace out the lines for the face, hands, or foldage of the
garments, for the leaves of your plants and feeds of flowers, or any
thing intended, in its proper shape made at first before the raiſed
work was laid, and according to which your Paſte was in ſuch manner directed, and confined by thoſe lines that were drawn as its
boundaries; for unleſs ſuch ſtroaks were made, 'tis impoſſible to
lave the paſte in its proper figure. This done, three or four small
inſtruments muſt be procured; one of them a bended Grayer, which
the Engravers make uſe of; the reſt, ſmall pieces of Steel, in ſhape
like a Chiſſel of the Carpenters, faſtened in a wooden handle, the
breadth of the largeſt, not exceeding a quarter of an inch, of the
others ſizeably leſs : With theſe your raiſed work muſt be cut,
ſcraped, and carved, leaving one part higher than the other, keeping due regard to the proportion of the thing you deſign. But here
I muſt forewarn you of the difficulty of the enterpriſe; no heavy,
ruſtick hand muſt be emploied in this tender, diligent work ; for if
in haſte or unadviſedly you attempt it , believe me your raiſed
work will break off in ſeveral places, to the diſgrace of the Artiſt,
and deformity of the piece. Let therefore your tools have an exquiſitely ſharp and ſmooth edge, whereby they may cut clean and
fine without roughneſs : And now 'tis time to ſmooth and ſleek
it with a bruſh that has been often uſed before, in order, in the laſt
place, to cloath it with any metal you ſhall judge moſt proper, as
ſhall hereafter be ſhewed at large.

The other way which we promiſed for raiſed work, is this: Strike
or trace out your deſign, as well the inſide as the outward ; that is,
the ſhape of your face, neck, hands, legs, the chief ſtroaks of the
foldings of the under and upper garments, ſo of flowers, or the like :
Then take your Paſte, ſomewhat thinner than you commonly uſe
it, and with it raiſe the lower garments or parts, which require the
leaſt raiſing. Grant it time to drie throughly, and then with a
very ſmall pencil dipt into the thickeſt of your Seed-Lace, varniſh
juſt the edges of your raiſed work ; for this intent, that when you

advance

advance the higher part, it may hinder the wet incorporating with the drie, which muſt be avoided; for ſhould it do ſo, the work will never ſhew well. This muſt be performed as often as you e- levate one part above another; and ſtill as your work is exalted, your paſte muſt be thicken'd; and raiſing each part ſucceſſively, beginning with the loweſt, you are to conclude with the upper- moſt; and when all is drie, if need require, ſmooth it with a ruſh, and then it is in a condition fit to receive your metal. Make rea- dy then what ſort of metal you pleaſe to cover it with, mixed in gum-water, and with a pencil deſtined for the uſe lay it on the raiſed work full and fair: give it leave to drie, and with a dogs tooth, which you may have at the Guilders, or a Stone or Agat, by them emploied in their Frames and Guilding, burniſh your work until it is bright, and ſhines as much as you deſire it ſhould. And farther, dip the pencil into your fineſt Lace-varniſh, and laie it over twice; then ſet it off, or ſhadow it with what your fancie di- rects, but of this I ſhall diſcourſe hereafter. Take notice, that if you grind more paſte than you can conſume at once, and it be drie before you ſhall have occaſion for it the ſecond time, grind it again, and tis fit for your buſineſs. You may judge of the ſtrength of your paſte, by the eaſie admittance of your nail preſs'd hard upon it, for then tis too weak, and muſt be hardened and ſtrengthened by a more ſtrong gum-water: Trials and Experience will give you more accurate, more ſatisfactorie directions. With theſe ingredi- ents, joined to Art and Skill, it is poſſible to make a paſte ſo hard, ſo ſtubborn, that a violent ſtroak with an hammer can neither break or diſcompoſe it.

CHAP. XII.

To prepare ordinary, rough-grain'd woods, as Deal, Oak, &c. whereby they may be Japanned, and look well.

PRovide ordinary Size, uſed by the Plaiſterers, and vended by Colour-ſhops, diſſolve it over the fire, making it pretty warm; mix Whiting with it until tis of a reaſonable body and conſiſtence, yet not too thick; then take a Bruſh fit for the purpoſe, made of hogs-hair. Lay your work once over with this mixture of Whit- ing and Size, and ſo often repeat it, until you have hid all the pores, crevices, and grain of your wood, ſuffering it to drie throughly between every turn. You may afterwards take a fine wet rag, and rub over your work, making it as ſmooth as your induſtry is able; this furbiſhing it with a cloath dipt in water, we call Water-plaining; when drie, ruſh it even and ſmooth, and as cloſe to the grain as poſſibly you can. This done, waſh over your work twice with the thickeſt of your Seed-Lace-varniſh; after

which,

which, if it be not smooth, again rush it, and in a day or so varnish
it over with black, or any other colour, as you have been directed
in those places where we have treated of it ; when it has stood sufficiently, you may apply your self to finish it by polishing.

According to these methods you are to prime carved Frames for
Cabinets or Chairs , when you desire they should look well ; with
this difference, that these must not be polisht, and by consequence
require not so great a body of varnish, no more than will contribute to a rich and splendid gloss. There is also another way, which
I recommend for the most valuable, because the most durable and
lasting, but not indeed of so large an extent as the former, being
proper only for the tops of Tables, Boxes, or the like ; and thus
you must proceed. Boil common Glew in water, let it be fine and
thin ; into which cast the finest Saw-dust, until tis indifferently
thick, and fit to lay with a brush, which you must provide for that
purpose. Run it over once with the glew so mixt ; if the grain of
the wood be not effectually obscured, wash it again, and two days
being given to harden, send it to a good workman or Cabinet-maker,
who must scrape it with his Scraper, as Pear-tree or Olive-wood are
served, and make it as fine and even as possibly he can ; then varnish it as you have been learn't to do by Pear-tree, or any other
smooth wood. This, if well done, will not come behind any for
beauty or durability. Tis confess'd, these labours are to be performed only upon cases of necessity, for they are very troublesom ;
and if every circumstance were truly weighed, not so cheap or valuable as your smooth, close-grained woods, of all which Pear-tree
is in the first place to be esteemed.

Of Bantam-work.

I Think it most proper in this place to speak of the manner of
working at Bantam, because the way of preparing the wood is
much the same with that of priming with Whiting. There are two
forts of Bantam as well as Japan-work: for as the Japan hath flat lying even with the black, and other lying high, like embossed work ;
so the Bantam hath flat also, and incut or carved into the wood, as
a survey of some large Screens, and other things that come from
those parts, will beyond all scruple convince and satisfie you : with
this difference however, that the Japan-Artist works most of all in
Gold, and other metals, the Bantam for the generality in Colours,
with a very small sprinkling of Gold here and there , like the
patches in a Ladies countenance. As for the flat work, it is done
in colours mixt with gum-water, appropriated to the nature of the
thing designed for imitation : for the ordering these colours with
gum-water, you have already received instructions. The carved or
in cut work, is done after this manner   Your Cabinet or Table,
                                                                    be

be it whatfoever you pleafe to work on, fhould be made of Deal, or fome other coarfe wood ; then take Whiting and Size, as before taught, lay it over your work, permitting it to drie between every wafh ; this muft be fo often done, till your primer or whiting lie almoft a quarter of an inch thick ; but always remember to mix your whiting and fize thinner than formerly, and lay it therefore over the oftner ; for if tis too thick, it will not only lie rough and unfeemly, but twill be apt to flie off and crackle. Having primed it to its due thicknefs, being drie, water-plain it, that is, as we hinted before, rub it with a fine, wet cloth ; in fome time after rufh it very fmooth ; lay on your blacks, and varnifh it up with a good body, and next of all in fome fpace polifh it fufficiently, though with a gentle and eafie hand. Being thus far advanced, trace and ftrike out your defign with vermilion and gum-water, in that very manner which you intend to cut and carve it, and very exactly ; your figures, Trees, Houfes, and Rocks, in their due proportions, with foldage of Garments, leafing of Trees, and in a word, draw it as if it were to ftand fo without any alteration. This finifhed, ex-ercife your Graver, and other inftruments, which are made of fhapes, differing according to each workman's fancie : with thefe cut your work deep or fhallow, as you think beft, but never carv-ing deeper than the whiting lies, for tis a great error to pafs through that and carve your wood, which by no means ought to feel the edg of your inftrument. Be mindful likewife to have black ftroaks for the draperie of garments, and the diftinction of one thing from another : as for example, if you were to work in this manner the great Bird, which is in the 11th Print at the end of this Book ; You ought, I fay, to carve where the white is, and leave the black untouch't, which fhews not only the feathering of the wings, but the form and fafhion of the Bird it felf ; the fame means are to be ufed in all other things which you undertake. But I fhould counfel that perfon, who defigns to imitate Bantam work, to endeavour to procure a fight of fome Skreen, or other piece ; for one fingle furvey of that will better inform him, than ten pages can inftruct or demonftrate. Had it been a thing of little trouble, or which might have been ufeful to the young and wil-ling practitioner, we had inferted a Plate or two of it, for it differs vaftly from the Japan in manner of draught ; but fince tis now al-moft obfolete, and out of fafhion, out of ufe and neglected, we thought it a thanklefs trouble and charge to affix a Pattern, which could neither advantage Us, or oblige You : I think no perfon is fond of it, or gives it houfe-room, except fome who have made new Cabinets out of old Skreens. And from that large old piece, by the help of a Joyner, make little ones, fuch as Stands or Tables, but never confider the fituation of their figures ; fo that in thefe things fo torn and hacked to joint a new fancie, you may obferve the fineft hodgpodg and medly of Men and Trees turned topfie tur-vie, and inftead of marching by Land you fhall fee them taking

I.

jour-

journeys through the Air, as if they had found out Doctor Wilkin-
son's way of travelling to the Moon; others they have placed in
such order by their ignorance, as if they were angling for Dolphins
in a Wood, or pursuing the Stag, and chafing the Boar in the middle of the Ocean : in a word, they have so mixed and blended the
Elements together, have made a league between fire and water, and
have forc't the clouds and mountains to shake hands, nay deprived
every thing of its due site and position, that if it were like any
thing, beside ruin and deformity, it must represent to you the
Earth, when Noah's Flood was overwhelming it. Such irregular
pieces as these can never certainly be acceptable, unless persons
have an equal esteem for uglie, ill-contrived works, because rarities
in their kind, as for the greatest performances of beautie and proportion.

But to return to our business.   When you have finished your
carved work, and cut it out clean and smooth, with your pencils
lay the colours, well and purely mixt, into your carved work, in
the manner which your ingenuity shall suggest, or the nature of it
absolutely require.   When the colours are finished, the gold may
be laid in those places where you have designed it, with powder-
gold, or brass-dust mixt with gum-water, but that looks not so
bright and rich as Leaf-gold, which the Bantam Artists always employ; and so may you also, if you make a very strong and thick
Gum-Arabick water, which you must laie with a pencil on your
work, and whilst it is wet take leaf-gold, cut it with a very sharp
smooth-edged knife (on a piece of leather straitly nail'd to a board)
in little pieces, shaped to the bigness and figure of the place where
you dispose of it.   Take it up with a little Cotton, and with the
same dab it close to the gum-water, and it will afford a rich lustre,
if your water be very strong; otherwise 'twill look starv'd and hun-
grie, when tis drie. Having thus finished your work, you must
very carefully clear up your black with oyl, but touch not your
colours, left you should quite rub them off, or soil them; for this
is not secured, as the other Bantam flat-work is; if wet come at
this, the colours will be ruined, and peel off. I confess I have
seen some even of the raised-work, whose colours would not stir,
but none so secured and firm as flat, in which you'll seldom or never find some Colours that will not endure a security with varnish, but with the loss of their native splendor : but those who
please may leave out the Taraishing colours, and secure their
carved work with a pencil, as formerly directed.

C H A P.

CHAP. XIV

To take off any Japan-patterns in this Book, upon any piece of work whatsoever.

VVHen your Black, or any other colour is varnished and polish't fit for draught, take a particular design out of this Book, or any thing else that is drawn upon paper, with whiting rub all over the back-side of your Print or Draught, and use a linnen cloth to wipe off all the whiting that lies rough and dusty on the back-side of your paper so whited. Then lay the Print on the Table or Box, with the whited side next to it, in the very place where you design the Draught should be made, and with a needle or piece of iron-wyer round and smooth at the point, fixed in a wooden handle for the purpose, not sharp to cut or scratch your Paper and Print, which we call a Tracing-pencil ; with this, I say, draw over and trace the Print as much as you think necessary, taking the most material and outward stroaks, or all others which you imagin are hard and difficult to draw without a pattern. This, by the assistance of the whiting with which your paper was rubb'd, will give the fashion and lines of what you have done, upon the Box or Table. After this, if you draw in Gold-size, use Vermilion mixt with Gum-water, and with a small pencil dipt in it, go over those lines made by the whiting ; for by this operation it will not easily come off, so that you may work at leisure with the Gold-size. But if you will work your metals or colours in gum-water, then trace or draw over your Design with Gum-water mixed with Brass or Gold-dust. Now either of these ways here mentioned, when drie and finished, will work either in Gum-water or Gold-size, as I have formerly discovered.

CHAP. XV.

The manner of working and setting off some Draughts in this Book:

I Think by this time I may truly say, That I have in a familiar and easie method proposed Rules for purchasing materials of all sorts, the manner of their composition, with the way of using Varnishes, laying of Metals, Colours, and whatsoever else is necessary, or may claim affinity and relation to the Varnishing and Japanning Art. But because these lines have a double design, to instruct and inform the ignorant, as well as assist those that have a

small

small knowledge and smattering in this Science: though I am perswaded I have sufficiently obliged the latter, yet because I may not be so clear and satisfactory in my Rules to those who before never attempted any thing of this nature, to whom tis a perfect Terra incognita, an undiscover'd Province; for their sakes I shall willingly make an addition of a few pages, to shew in a plain and more particular manner the way of working some Patterns in this Book either in Metals or Colours, by the knowledge whereof they may be enabled with ease and inclination to perform any enterprize that shall oppose them. To these I shall affix the different ways of setting off and adorning your work, which I have before rather mentioned and touch't upon, than treated of.

The first eight Copper-prints, at the end of this Book, are several designs for small work, of whose differences their Titles will inform you: Two others for Drawers of Cabinets; one, of all sorts of Birds flying in Antick figures; two, of Birds great and less, standing in various postures; another of Beasts, &c. Two figures of Chinese men and women, in untoward gestures, and habits: Others, of Flower-pots, Sprigs, Trees, and the like: Lastly, their Temples, Structures, and Palaces; their manner of worship, and reception of foreign Ministers and Embassadors; with as much pleasing variety as can reasonably be expected. Any part of these may be placed on the work, as the fancy and ingenuity of the undertaker shall direct: yet I shall give a little light after what manner they may be transposed.

Suppose then you have a large piece of work, as a Table, or Cabinet; take one of the Prints which chiefly complies with your humour, insert others also which may be most agreeable, yet give variety too: borrow a part from one, a figure from another, birds flying or standing from a third; this you may practise until your Cabinet be sufficiently charged: if after all this any thing be wanting, your judgment must order, beautifie, and correct. But observe this always, that if you would exactly imitate and copie out the Japan, avoid filling and thronging your black with draught and figure, for they, as you may remark, if ever you happen to view any of the true Indian work, never croud up their ground with many Figures, Houses, or Trees, but allow a great space to little work: And indeed tis much better, and more delightful; for then the Black adds lustre to the Gold, and That by way of recompence gives beautie to the Black.

But here an Objection may be started; That if a little work is most natural, and according to the Pattern which the Indians have set us, why have not I followed that Rule in my Draughts annexed to this Book? To this I answer; That if I had so done, I must have provided thrice the number of Plates, to shew the variety that these have sufficiently done; not to mention a triple charge that would have attended. Again, should these have been
beau-

beautified with little work, I had then been liable to cenfure for being niggardly of my Patterns, and depriving the practitioner of choice and variety: But by what I have prefented, I have fecurely failed between this Scylla and Charybdis; have paffed the Rock on one hand, and the Gulph on the other; and, if I am not flattered, have not only obtained the good liking of the Curious, but fuffici-ently fupplied the wants of thofe who are great undertakers. Here you may alter and correct, take out a piece from one, add a frag-ment to the next, and make an entire garment compleat in all its parts, though tis wrought out of never fo many difagreeing Pat-terns. Befides, I have not by this variety fixt a Ne plus ultra to your fancie, but have left it free, and unconfined: I do advife that no one would oblige himfelf to keep clofe to the Copy, for even the fmall Cutts will fupply the place of a much larger Box than is there exprefs'd, and not injure or difgrace it. I do with modefty and fubmiffion pretend not to confine, but lead and affift your fancie. Thus much in general terms; I'le detain you no lon-ger on this large and pregnant Topick, but regularly now defcend to particulars, and inftruct you how to work off fome of the fore-mentioned Draughts.

To work the First Draught.

This affords you ornaments for the tops and fides of little Boxes; which, when traced out according to the directions already given, muft be done with gold, if you work in gum-water: Take your gold-fhell, and with your pencil fill fome of the tops of your houfes; and thofe parts which you obferve in your Print to be mark't with black lines, as the Doors, Windows, &c, afterwards the Sprigs, Flowers, and Birds, all of them in a fair, fmall, but full ftroak: now if you paint thefe latter things with colours, they may be va-rioufly managed, with red, fome others with blew, a third with filver, until the whole be entirely compleated. If you think to raife any of thefe, be fure to practife on thofe that lie firft and foremoft, for which I do refer you to the Chapter of Raifed work.

When you have thus far advanced, tis required that you fhould proceed to Setting off, which I defire now to make my bufinefs to inform you, as having never yet mentioned it; yet I fhall at pre-fent confine it only to that of Gum-water, for this is not the way with Gold-fize, of which more properly hereafter. When the leaves and tops of your Houfes are fairly laid in Flat-work; to make the black and fhining veins of your leaves, the tiling of your buildings, and foldage of garments, appear through your gold and metals, as fome of the Indian work does, exercife your Tracing-pencil, breathing on your work with your mouth clofe to it; and when moiftened with your breath, ftreak or draw out the veins and foldage of the figures, their hands, face, and parts fo made in their proper order. When your metal begins to drie, and will not feparate, force it to part again by breathing on it, for that moift-

nefs

ness will reduce it to obedience, which must be observed too in a
moderate degree; for if you make it over-wet and damp, the trac-
ing-iron tis true will disjoin it, yet no sooner can it pass the place
but it closes up, and reduces it self to its former amicable conjunction; as a Ship that ploughs and divides the Sea, makes a chan-
nel in an instant, but as that sails off the waters return, the breach
is healed, and the place of its passage is no more to be found. Too
much moisture is therefore as great an inconvenience as none at
all. Perhaps your work may be rough and unhandsom before tis
throughly drie, yet after that, a soft, new pencil by brushing will
cast off that disguise, will command the loose rough particles to
withdraw, and represent the Veinings and Hatchments in a smooth
and pleasant dress.

To set off Raised work with Black.

When your Raised work has been varnished and burnished, put
Lamp-black into a Mussel-shell, and with gum-water hardly wet
it, for if you allow it too large a portion, you'l find it a difficult
task to make it comply and incorporate: but when it is mixt,
which you must perform with your brush, then add as much water as will prepare and enable it, by the assistance of a small well-
pointed pencil, to draw fine black stroaks. These must frame the
lineaments and features of the Faces, the foldage of your raised
Figures, the veins of Leaves, Seeds, the bodies of Trees, together
with the black hatchments of your Flowers. If you would have
any Rocks speckled, first pass them over with the said black, and
when dry, grant them two washes with the Securing-varnish; lastly, lay on the Speckles. One thing here deserves your observation;
If your good will and labour cannot be accepted, and your black, or
whatsoever you Set off with, will not be received; pass over the
Raised work with a Tripolee-cloth in a soft and gentle manner, lest
the Metals should be seduced, and forsake their apartment.

This manner of Setting off is more practised than that with a
Tracing-pencil, or breathing on it, not only for Raised but Flat-
work too; for when your piece is drie, salute it once with the Securing-varnish, after which take your black pencil, and employ it
in hatching and veining at your own pleasure; other metals and
colours desire the same management: I will give you an instance;
if a red flower were to be Set off with Silver, then must your Red
be secured with varnish: and being first supposed to drie, hatch and
vein it with your Silver. These directions must be of force and
consequence in all cases where you design to work one thing on another, whether colour upon metal, metal upon colour, or metal
upon metal, without being guilty of false Heraldrie. Having adorned and Set off your piece, if it be Flat-work, you may make use
of the varnish spoken of in the 13th page of this Book, to secure
your whole piece both draught and ground-work, which will endure polishing: but if for Raised-work, you must make use of
                                                        the

the other Securing-varnish, which is set down in the 12th page, and
the reason is , because your Rais'd-work will not bear a polish as
the other, but must only be secured, and cleared up. But here is
to be noted, that this last varnish may be used either for Flat, or
Raised-work, but the former is only proper for Flat. In working
with Gum-water be ever vigilant and careful that your metals or
colours be not too strong of gum , for it will utterly spoil their
beautie and complexion; but when you have sufficiently mixed
them in the beginning , fair water afterward may quench their
drought. Look upon this as a general, unerring guide; let them
be just so far encouraged with gum, as may oblige them to stick
close to your work, and enable them to endure varnishing without
coming off: If this should at last prove a repetition, you must pardon me; tis a business that I am very zealous for, and should be
highly concerned to think of a miscarriage, in the last, ornamental
part of the undertaking; and if you strictly examin it, you'l find,
if this is not new altogether, yet it may bear a second reading , as
being a paraphrase and explanation of the former.

I intimated before, that the Rocks should be last of all treated
of, because not to be finished till the rest were compleated; only
those few scattered sprigs, supposed to grow out of them, that they
may not appear bald and naked, nor too full of 'em, lest they might
confound the eye, and interrupt the shadow. Now if these Rocks
are to be covered with metals, with your pencil lay Gold, Silver,
or Copper, in a full body round the outward stroaks, which were
traced with your pencil, in breadth a quarter of an inch; prevent
its being too wet; call for a large Goose-quill-pencil, cut off the
point, making it flat and blunt at the end: With this touch or
dab your Metal, then do the like to the black part of the Rock,
whereby that may be sprinkled with some of the metal too, by little and little continue it until the whole be scattered over; yet
these Specks should be thicker towards the sides and top, than in
the middle. Other metals, artificial and adulterate, may be laid
according to these directions, and may be dabb'd or workt with your
middle finger as well as the Goose-pencil. Thus much may suffice
for the first Print, workt in Gum-water : I shall give some brief directions how to proceed in some few more ; for by understanding
those, you may safely adventure on any that remain.

The Second Pattern.

This is a representation of Birds, which if you work with gold
and colours, I advise that the body of the first Bird, that stands before the other, be done in gold, the wings with bright copper, and,
when secured, let its breft be redded a little with vermilion, in that
part of it which in the Print is darker than the rest. Then take
your black shell, and beautifie the eye , and the touches about it
with black ; as also the feathering of the body and the back. Let

M 2   the

the wing be set off or feathered with silver, the long black stroaks
in the feathers of it with black; the tail, legs, and bill with gold,
but change the white lines in the tail for black. The bodies of the
other Birds may be laied with adulterate, dirtie, dark copper, but
the wings gold, set off the body with the same; the brest with
touches of silver, the wing with black: Lastly, let the tail be
bright copper, and feathered with white, the bill and feet gold.
Next, cover the Flies body with gold, his wings with bright copper, hatcht or set off with silver, the body with black. Make your
Bird on the second Box-lid with gold, feather and shadow it with
bright gold; let the wing be with vermilion and Lamblack mixt,
till tis become a dirtie red; feather it with gold, the quills with
silver, the beak gold, and the legs vermilion. Let the other Bird
be gold in the body, feathered about the wing (as you may see in
the Pattern) with black; the wing natural copper, feathered with
white or silver; let the Flies be gold, and set them off with black.
Beautifie the first Bird, on the lid of the Patch-box, with bright or
red copper; hatch it with silver, touch it about the eye and head
with black; make the wing of gold, feathered with black; the
feet and bill of the same metal. The other Bird behind it must
have green gold in the body, feathered with silver; the wing gold
as the other, hatcht with black. On the other lid make the Bird
gold, the wings bright red copper, feathered with white and toucht
with black. The sides of each box may be contrived after the same
manner: the sprigs deserve all to be laid in gold, as the rocks with
different metals, and shadowed, but allow the outward stroaks to
be gold, not only as they confine, but as they adorn your work.

The Third Draught.

Before this piece can be adventured on, you are desired thus to
make a paint or colour for the face and hands of the Figures. Grind
white-lead finely on your Marble-stone; add as much Auripigment
or Orpiment, as will give it a tawny colour; if you think it too
lively and bright, allay it with Lamblack, which may contribute
to a swarthy complexion, and nearest the Indian: but if you are
inclined rather to a pleasant, flesh-like colour, a little vermilion
or dragons-blood mixed with it, can to any degree oblige you. Now
if you love variety of figures, you may use as many mixtures for
their countenances; and distinguish the Master from the man, the
Abigail from the Mistress by her tawnie skin. Lay then the garment of your Figure in the first powder-box-lid in bright red copper;, on that part which covers the breft, and encircles the neck,
paint vermilion; let the cap and stick be of gold: set off the foldage of his vesture with silver, and close to each silver-thread join
other of black; set off the black with the same. Lastly, strike out
the lineaments of the face, and shapes of the hands, with black also:
Let his Lacquey, the boy that attends him, have a golden livery,
the

the bundle under his arm red, with a cap of silver. Set off the garment and cap with black, his parcel with lines of silver. Order the Bird and Flie to be overlaid with gold, and set off with black As for your Sprig, the great leaves must be green gold and pale copper, border'd with bright gold; your flowers vermilion, encompassed with silver, and seeded with the same; garnish the small leaves and stroaks with gold. The cover to the second Box should have its first figure attired in gold, where the black surrounds his neck, vermilion, the forepart of the cap the same, the hinder gold; his vest buttoned, looped, and drapered with black; the red of the cap and neck edged with silver, the gold of the cap hatcht with black; the feet bright copper, set off with silver. The other gentleman his companion, that he may have as good apparrel as his friend, let his cap before be gold, behind green gold; set off the first part with black, the latter with silver, the covering for his neck with the same metal; his long robe will require green gold, set off with bright gold; his feet of the same, set off with black. The Flie and Bird just as the former, the Sprig in like manner, except the seed, gold, set off with black. The Figure in the first Patch-box may be arrayed in bright copper, hatched or set off with silver; the cap and staff gold, the tree also. The figure on the other little box should have his upper coat vermilion, hatcht with silver; the under gold, set off with black; the stick, bird, and flie, gold; his feet, the colour of his face: The sprig, all gold, except the flowers, which may be red and silver, set off with black and silver. Let the sides be all gold, saving the rocks, which may be silver and copper.

Thus have I directed you in these methods of working colours, and how sparingly I have made use of them, for the least part of them is sufficient: and unless even these are workt clean, and with good judgment, it were more credit to omit, than insert 'em. But because some have a particular genius and inclination that way, I shall not make this Tract so incompleat as to forsake the treatise of them, and therefore to oblige universally the next Section is subjoined.

How to work in Colours and Gold the great Sprig in the XIIIth Print.

This has infinite variety, and by consequence will require the aid and assistance of very many colours, so that the Transparent ones may be here emploied as well as the others.

First therefore trace out your design, and fill most part of the small work belonging to it, as the stems and little leaves, with gold, passing by however a few of them, to be reserved for bright copper, green gold, or the like; added too in such sort, that they may grace and enliven the piece: for tis the custom and fashion of the Japan-artificers, to fill frequently with dead metals, yet bind 'em in with gold. From these set upon the great leaves and flowers in the posture that they lie, and fill 'em by these directions, or any

N   others

others of the like kind. But by way of example; The firſt great
flower next the rock, half covered by great Leaves lying before it,
I would fill the ſeeded part with ſilver, the leaves with vermilion,
and in ſetting off, work it in black Diamond-wiſe, and thoſe little
ſpots of black which lie lurking in the white, with bright red copper ; then the part that is fill'd with red, I ſhould bind in with
ſilver, and vein it with the ſame. From this I come to the other
on the right hand, and fill the ſeed of that flower with bright copper, the leaves with ſilver, and when I come to ſet off, border the
ſeed with black, the inſide with ſilver, compaſs in the leaves with
gold, hatching them with black. From hence I march to that on
the left, partly hid by a great leaf: the ſeed of this ſhall be green
gold, its ſquares bright gold , the ſpots in the ſquares vermilion,
its leaves with dark heavy copper, ſet off with ſilver. Next for the
three flowers that lie ſomewhat above this : that in the middle I
would do with green gold, the ſeed bright gold, ſquared with black:
the other may be laid with ſilver, ſeeded with bright copper, hatcht
and ſquared with black. The laſt with vermilion , the ſeeds with
tranſparent green, and encloſe them with vermilion, and hatch
in the leaves with ſilver. From theſe I would proceed to the o-
ther flower, oppoſite to them on the right hand, ſomewhat larger ;
whoſe ſeed muſt be red, bound in and chequer'd with ſilver, covering the leaves with blew, hatcht and ſurrounded with gold : the
little one above that with red, the ſeed with blew, ſet off with ſilver. From theſe we make our progreſs to the two great flowers
above them : the firſt may be laid with tranſparent blew, bounded
and worked with gold, the leaves covered with ſilver, and hatcht
with vermilion : the ſeed of the ſecond with dirty copper, ſet off
and encircled with ſilver ; the leaf of the ſaid flower cloathed with
deep bright red copper, hatcht with black. Next buſie your ſelf
in filling the ſingle great flower above that, whoſe ſeed may be dirty gold, environed and ſquared with ſilver ; the ſpots in the ſquares
done with bright gold , that part of the leaves that is white
changed for black, and with gold hide the black that lies in the
white : the remaining part of the leaf may be laid with bright red
copper, bounded with ſilver, and hatcht with the ſame. As for
the flower next above that, I would lay the ſeed in tranſparent red,
ſet it off with ſilver, border it vvith black ; then make the leaves
ſilver, and hatch it vvith black. Afterward, the three above this ,
I vvould work in the ſame manner vvith the lovvermoſt three ;
but that above all, may have his ſeed bright copper , compaſſed
and ſet off vvith black ; the leaves dirty copper, vvhich might be
hatcht and encloſed vvith vvhite. Novv remember, I beſeech you,
that although I have mentioned filling and ſetting off together, for
the more eaſie apprehenſion of it, yet be conſtantly mindful to lay
all your plain colours, before you think of ſetting them off ; and
the reaſon of it is this, becauſe you are more ready to ſet off vvith
one colour, before you undertake another, and your fancie is more
quick

quick and ready to adorn and garnish every single flower and leaf. Now supposing the flowers filled, let us contrive what shall be the covering of the great leaves. But to be brief: Deck them with metals, generally such as green, dirtie gold; pale, muddy copper; yet intermix here and there blew and green transparent: bound and vein 'em with such as give the greatest life; not wild, gawdy colours, so much as grave, modest, and delightful. I advise you sometimes to double your borders in the leaves, with the ground-black of the Box or Table left between, as the Print will inform you: And again, make all your veins, finishing lines, and the stroaks you set off with, fine, clean, even, and smooth. By this time I suppose, whosoever shall survey these last pages, may imagine we have pleased our selves with fancies and Chimæra's, that we have discours'd like men in a dream; nothing but Gold, Silver, and the richest colours can satisfie our luxuriant fancies; nay, we pretend to have it in such plenty too, that Solomon himself, compared to us, was a beggar: By our talk we are Masters of both Indies, Pactolus Sands, and the Mountains of Potosi should be our proper inheritance; for, like Midas, and the Philosophers stone, we turn every thing to Gold.   Our Birds are so splendidly arrayed, that all common ornaments are excluded; the best Dyes so universally overspread their wings, that you'd imagin they would outshine the Bird of Paradise. The clothing and livery of the Fields are mean and heavy, when compared to the Flowers our Art has produced, whose lustre is more radiant, more durable, and surprizing.

CHAP. XVI.

To work in Gold-size the Twentieth Print of this Book.

Since our Gentry have of late attained to the knowledge and distinction of true Japan, they are not so fond of colours, but covet what is rightly imitated, rather than any work beside, tho never so finical and gawdy. The most excellent therefore in this Art copy out the Indian as exactly as may be in respect of Draught, Nature, and Likeness; in this performance then colours must be laid aside. Some variety of metals indeed may be admitted, but in a very slender proportion to that of gold, which is the Fac totum, the general ornament of right genuine Japan-work. This undertaking now in hand may be done with gold only; But I shall in the next Chapter choose a Print, whereon perfect and corrupt metals may be laid. To begin therefore with that of Gold: Be ever cautious and exact when you trace or draw out your design in vermilion or gold; which being performed with an even hand, call for your gold-size, ready prepared for the draught; use a small

con-

convenient pencil, to mark in your fize the outward lines, the
boundaries of that rock, which in the twentieth Print you may
perceive lies beyond the Buildings ; and although you do begin
here, you are not to fill it (either with metals or fpeckles,) until
the other work is concluded ; for, if you remember, we charged
you before, to finifh the Rocks in the laft place. Again, if I may
counfel you, begin with the remoteft part, that which is fartheft
diftant from you ; for then you will not be liable to the inconvenience of rubbing, or defacing any thing whilft it is wet, with an unwelcom hand, or intruding elbow. Having therefore in fhort un-
dertaken the fartheft part firft, work it juft as the Print is ; I mean,
draw your gold-fize on the black lines of the Print, and no where
elfe ; referving the white for the black Japan or ground of your
Table. But to explain it a litle more : In all refpects operate with
your Size, as if you were to copy the Print on white paper with
ink, or black Lead ; only take care, that whilft you are buried in
working one part, you fuffer not that already done with fize to drie
to that degree, that it will not receive and embrace your metal,
but very often try the draught fo lately made : if it is clammy,
and fticks fomewhat to your finger, but not fo as to bring off any,
then tis high time with your leather to lay and rub on the gold-
duft : if it clings to your finger fo faft, as to come off with it, then
know it is not fufficiently drie ; if tis no way clammy, you may
conclude tis too ftubborn for the reception of the metal. This ca-
veat, being rightly managed, fet upon your drawing part again, and
fo continue, now making lines, then guilding them, until the
whole be compleated. If you find it a tedious, troublefome undertaking to draw the white, and pafs over the black ; or, on the contrary, to draw the black and omit the vvhite on the tops of your
houfes, or foldage of figures, faces, or the like ; then for your cafe
overlay all thofe parts of your building or foldage &c with gold-
fize, and when your metal is laid on that, and is well dried, wafh
over with Securing-varnifh thofe places only which you defign to
fet off with black : which done, exercife your pencil in making
thofe lines and divifions that are required to diftinguifh the parts
of your houfe, as the Tiling, Draperie of garments, or any thing
of the like nature. The reafon why we enjoin you to wafh with
varnifh, is not out of any fufpition or jealoufie that the fize or
metal will forfake its allotted feat, but becaufe its furface is generally too fmooth and greafie to admit of and unite with the black,
unlefs reconciled by the mediation of the aforefaid varnifh. What
I have propounded is an example for any other Print, that you
could wifh or defire to accomplifh in Gold-fize : and indeed I had
been very negligent, fhould I have permitted this noble fubject to
reft in filence and oblivion ; this, which above all others prefents
us with the grandeur and majefty of Japan.work ; our under-per-
formances vanifh and fhrink away, when the Mafter-piece is expofed to view. Let the narrow-foul'd Mifer hug and adore his

bags

bags, and pray to the golden Calf that he has erected, I shall neither envy or comply with his idolatry; for I had rather line my House with that precious metal, than my Coffers.

CHAP. XVII.

To work in Gold-size the twentythird Print of this Book, with perfect or corrupt Metals.

THis draught requires a greater variety of colours than any of the precedent, without which it were no mean or ordinary performance to dress every figure in its proper habit, and equippe the attendance according to their respective qualities ; but to shew what Art and Contrivance can effect, we have on purpose selected this Pattern, which was chiefly designed for colours, and intend to alter the property, converting it to perfect and mixt metals : so that if we overcome the most difficult, all meaner undertakings must by consequence yeild obedience and submission. Were I therefore allowed to prescribe in this affair, I would in the first place overlay the canopy and curtains belonging to it with pure gold, then flower, and set them off with black : the two streamers or flags may be done in bright copper, faintly shadowed with powder-Tin, or dirtie silver; for the best and brightest silver is to glaring a metal for black Japan, and very seldom if ever made use of, (yet I must acknowledge I have seen several Cabinets of Raised-work come from the Indies wrought altogether in Silver, but that is not authority sufficient for us to practise it in Gold-work.) As for the King, his face and hands should not be of the ordinary hue with inferior mortals ; Gold best becomes his Majesties countenance, his eyes and beard black, his cap green gold set off with bright gold; his body may be cloathed in bright red copper, shadowed with black ; the table-cloth covered with green gold, shadowed or set off with bright. The figure kneeling by him, should have his upper garment done in dirtie gold, shadowed faintly with dirtie silver, but his under in Powder-tin, hatcht with black ; his feet with dirty copper. The bottom of the Throne, with the Ascent, you are to lay with gold, and set it off with black : The Ambassador first in rank approaching the throne, may be allowed the same metal for his face with his Majesty, and set off as his too with black ; that on his shoulders and sleeves with bright red copper, shadowed with black ; his present in his hand, gold, his cap green-gold, set off with bright ; his feather behind it bright copper, set off with black ; his body dirtie copper, shadowed faintly with dirty silver, or tin, yet flowered with bright gold; his feet bright copper, set off with black. The figure immediately following him I should clad in gold ; the cap may be bright copper, all shadowed or

O   set fet off with black; his prefent in his hand, his fhoos and girdle, bright copper fet off with black. The third Gentleman's face, hands, and feet, I would work in natural copper fet off with black, that on his head powder-tin fhadowed with black; the covering on his fhoulders green-gold, fpotted and hatched with bright gold. His outward apparrel fhould be a lay of bright copper, fet off with black; that in his hand, gold; his under-veftment the fame, and hatch it with black. The laft figure may have his hands, face, and feet, covered with gold, fet off with black; the upper-garment with green-gold, flowered and fet off with bright gold; the under, natural copper fet off with black; that on his fhoulder with bright, red copper, fhadowed alfo with black. The body of the tree can be done with dirty gold, fhadowed and fet off as you fee with bright gold; the leaves of the fame. Laftly, the fruit, bright copper, and hatcht with black.

Thus may you work with Metals only, and vary it according to your fancie. And you may fet off your plain metals, when rubbed on Gold-fize, either with Metals mixed with Gum-water, or Gold-fize; that is, when your plain Metals are layed, and throughly drie, hatch or work in the Size for fetting off, as you would do with Metals mixed with Gum-water. You may ufe which you pleafe, but tis my opinion that Gold-fize is beft.

I had rather fee an Embaffy thus in Miniature, than take a voyage into China that I might really behold one: not that we have too richly attired his Majefty, and the Ambaffadors, or given them more magnificent habiliments than ever they beftowed upon themfelves. Whether the King is defired to join in the league againft the Tartar, or to ftand Neuter, I cannot truly determine; but by thofe weighty reafons, the Golden Prefents, we conjecture that he may be bribed, and brought over to the party. The Agent feems very zealous in the bufinefs; what will be the iffue and event, lies not in my power to foretel at prefent; nay, if you fhould have patience to tarry till the revolution of the Platonick year, when every thing fhall be in the fame pofture it is now, even then by confequence we fhould be ignorant of it. This indeed I can affure you, I have known thefe Politicians nigh ten years, and never faw them yet in any other manner than what the Picture reprefents; and do therefore imagin, that there are no hopes of an amicable and fudden conclufion.

We however fhall novv fix a period to this Treatife of Japan, as you may perceive by our giddy difcourfe, vvhich feems to imply, that vve have nothing more to fay to the purpofe. Yet give me leave, kind Reader, to offer fomething before vve take our formal leaves of this fubject. Many excellent Arts are buried in oblivion, vvhich muft certainly be afcribed to the neglect of the skilful, vvho never committed them to pofterity by the ufeful conveyveyance of Manufcript or the Prefs ; Painting of Glafs , and making it malleable, may ferve for inftances of Arts that have mifcarried, either through the lazinefs or ill nature of the Artifts, who would not communicate their ingenuity to after-ages, or elfe through envy denied it a longer date than themfelves, and foolifhly refolved it fhould not furvive them. Short-fighted ignorants ! as if their fame and memory could die whilft their Arts thrived, or that their great Grand-fons fhould admire the invention, without entertaining a juft efteem and deference for its Author. Yet I would not have you miftake me, and furmife, that I have made a circular Preamble, to hook my felf into the circumference ; for I propofed this Tract as a means to perpetuate my Art only. I muft confefs, I have too great an Efteem for this Pallas of mine, then in the leaft to flight or neglect it ; and I think my felf obliged to make as good a provifion for the iffue of my Brain, as that of my Body ; for the firft is entirely my own, but I am forc't to admit of a Partner in the generation of the latter. I fhall never be follicitous for my felf, and look upon Applaufe to be as empty and infignificant after death as before it ; and am not in the leaft ambitious to live by another's breath, when I am deprived of my own. If I may be allowed to beftow a hearty Wifh, it muft be for its Succefs, that it may flourifh and be admired ; that from thefe lines, as from the Serpents teeth which Cadmus fowed, may fpring experienced Artifts, that will inveft it with fplendor and reputation ; yet with this difference from the parallel, that they may mutually confpire to eftablifh and eternize it.

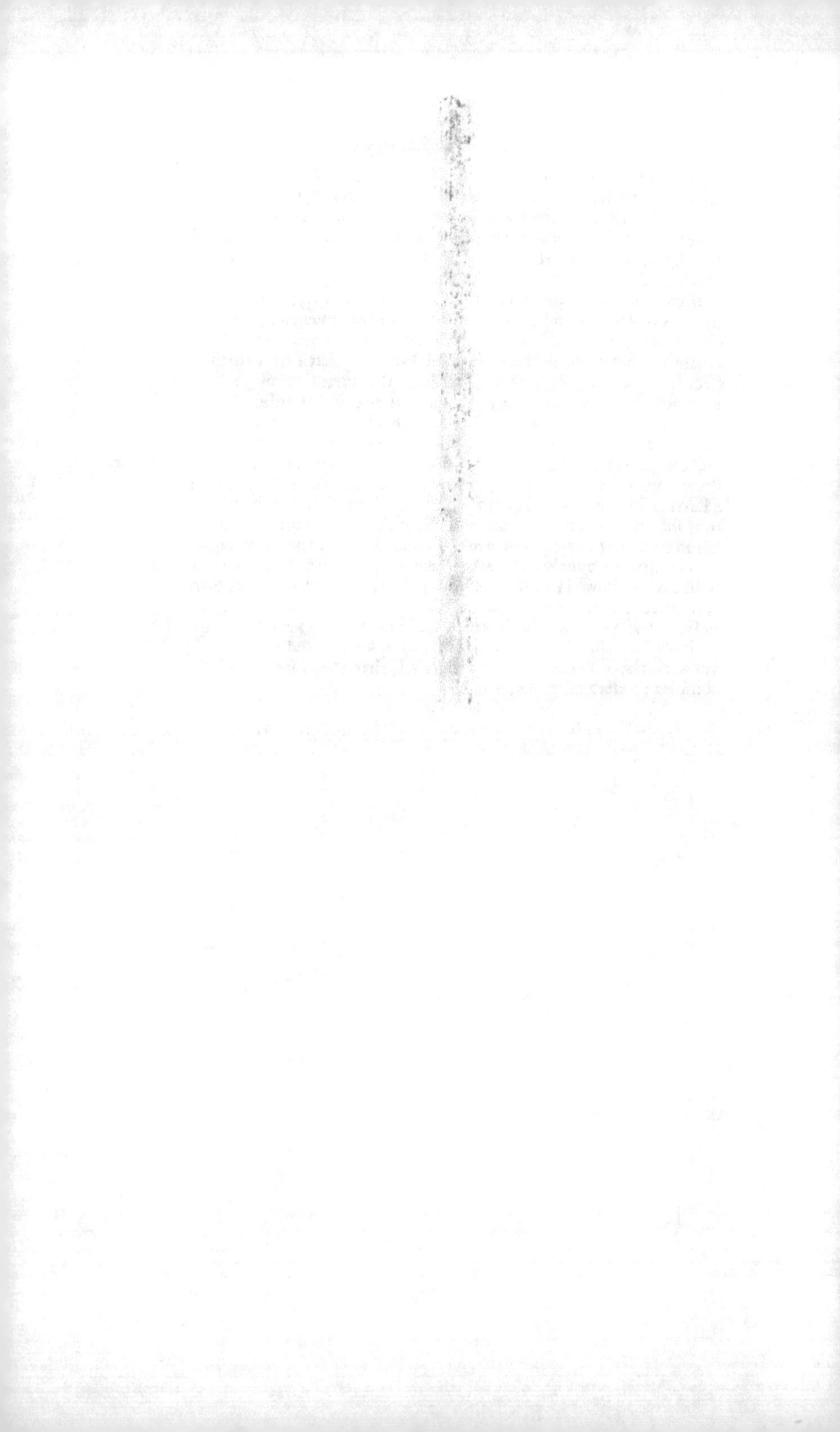

THE ART OF
GUILDING, LACKERING, &c,
display'd.

CHAP. XVIII.

To guild any thing in Oyl, whereby it may safely be exposed to the weather.

VVE have hitherto uttered big and glorious words, hardly a Page that has not ecchoed Gold and Silver ; but if you'l pardon us, we will frankly and ingeniously confess, that the expressions are as valuable as the things : for Brass-dust, and viler metals have been thus disguised to counterfeit the more noble and excellent : yet it cannot be denied, but that they are such cunning cheats as may almost impose upon the skilful and ingenious. And this may be said in their behalf, That although they deceive the eye, they neither pick or endanger the purse , which true gold would do after a most profuse and unnecessary manner. Well then by way of requital we shall cast away the vizor, and lay aside the mimick dress ; for the Art now in hand will not admit of the former couzenage. Guilding accepts not of base materials, is wholly unacquainted with dross or allay, and the finest unadulterate gold is the only welcom and acceptable guest. I am sensible that the Guilders on metals will quarrel at the name, who pretend, that Guilding is a term appropriated to the working on Metals only ; but the dispute is equally trivial, and unreasonable : for if I overlay Wood or any other body with Gold, I cannot conceive how I transgrefs the rules of common sense or English , if I say, I have guilded such a wood ; and I shall therefore acquiesce in this title, until the frivolous Enquirers furnish me with a more natural and proper appellation. However, since some of that profession have upon this occasion disputed the title with me, though to no purpose, to shew that I can and will be as good as my word , I'le give you their way of Guilding of Metals in full to end the dispute. But to the business in hand : I shall here instruct you in all things necessary for this way of Guilding, as Primer, Fat Oyl, and Gold-size, all which are to be gotten at the Colour-shops. Priming may be

P   as-

afforded for 6d. the pound, the other two will coft each of them 3d the ounce: but becaufe they are fearce commodities, and feldom to be met with very good, tis requifite for thofe who guild much, to make it themfelves, alter this manner.

To make Priming.

Priming you may make of any colour that hath a body; as white-lead, brown or red Oker, and Umber, ground in oyl pretty light: but the Painters have the beft conveniency for this compofition; for tis made of the fcraping of their pots, the oldeft skinny colours, and the cleanfing or filth of their Pencils. All thefe being mixed grind very well, put them into a canvas-bag that will hold a pint, fowed very ftrongly for this purpofe. If the colour be too dark, it may be alter'd by adding a little white-lead. Being fecurely in-clofed and tied up, prefs it between a pair of Screws, fuch as Apo-thecaries employ, now and then turning the bag, until all the fine primer be fqueezed out, which fhould be received into a Gallipot, the skins and filth that remain are ufelefs, and may therefore be thrown away. With this your piece muft be very thinly primed over, and permitted to drie.

Fat Oyl

Is nothing elfe but Linfeed oyl, managed thus. Put it into leaden veffels, fhaped like dripping-pans, but fo, that the oyl may not be above an inch deep. Set them out expofed to the Sun for five or fix months, until it become as thick as Turpentine, the longer it ftands the more fat it will be, and by confequence the Gold will re-quire a better glofs; if it arrive to the confiftence of butter, that it may be almoft cut with a knife, referve it carefully, and as the beft for ufe that can poffibly be made.

Gold-Size in Oyl.

Provide the beft yellow Oaker, fee it very finely grinded and thick with Linfeed-oyl, which is fomething fat. This done confine them to a pipkin, and put on it fome fat oyl, to keep it from skinning over: cover it with paper, or a bladder to guard it from duft and injury; lay it afide for your occafions. You may ufe it prefently, and if you keep it feven years twill come to no damage, but on the contrary be much better for your purpofe. Should it happen that you might have old gold-fize that is skinny, and yellow and brown Oaker in the fame condition, grind them, fhut them up in a clean Canvas bag; prefs it between your Screw as your Primer was, un-til you have made a feparation, and parted the good and ferviceable from the bad and infignificant; a Gallipot is a fit receptacle for the firft, and the dunghil for the latter. This fort of Gold-fize is ready to ferve your prefent and more urgent neceffities; if you defire to have a piece extraordinary, I advife you to prime it thinly over once more, allowing it four or five days to drie, if your bufinefs will permit, if not, inftead thereof Lacker over your work in the
                                                                          Sun

Sun, or some such moderate heat, and then tis rightly prepared for the reception of the Gold-fize.

Take of the best Gold-fize, and of fat Oyl, an equal quantity, yet no more than your piece requires. Mix and incorporate them well together by the means of your Stone and Muller, and put them into a pot; procure a clean Brush that has been formerly used, and with it dipt in the Size pass over all the piece very thinly, jobbing and striking the point of the pencil into the hollow places of the carved work, that no place, creek, or corner of your work may escape the salutation ; for every part of your Frame or thing that hath not been partaker of the Gold-fize, or touched with it, is not in a condition to embrace or receive your Leaf-gold ; so that if care in this be wanting, your work, when it comes to be guilt, will be full of faults, and look scurvily. Having thus done, remove it to a convenient place for twenty four hours, free and secure from dust ; the longer it stands, the better glofs your Gold or Silver will be adorned with, provided that it be tacky and clammy enough to hold your metals. Now to distinguish the true exact time when the Gold-fize is fit to be guilded, breath on it ; if your breath covers it over like a mist, tis evident that you may lay on your Gold ; or otherwise, prefs your finger upon it somewhat hardly ; and if you perceive tis so drie, that it will neither difcolour or stick to your finger, but is in some meafure clammy, tacky, and unwilling to part with it, conclude tis in a good condition : should you attempt to guild before the Size is drie enough, that moisture will drown and deprive your Gold of that glofs and luftre which it would acquire if skilfully performed ; on the contrary, if the Size is over-drie, you are come too late, you have loft the opportunity, for it will not accept of the Gold. The first mifcarriage of being too moist, is rectified by suffering it to stand one day longer to drie ; the latter, which is so drie and stout, that it will not receive it, must be confined to a damp cellar for a night, and then without question twill willingly accept of the golden Bribe.

You are defired in the first place to furnish your felf with a Cuhion made of Leather stufft very even with Tow, and strained on a board 10 inches one way, and 14 the other. On this you are to cut the gold and filver with a thin, broad, sharp, and smooth-edged knife : To thefe, three or four Pencils of finer hair than ordinary ; some are of Swans-quills, and fold fingly for 6d. the Artifts ufe also the end of a Squirrels tail fpread abroad, and fastened to a flat pencil-stick, which is broad at one end, and fplit, juft like an houfe-painter's Graining-tool, but lefs ; it ferves for taking up and laying on whole Leaves at a time, and is by them called a Pallet Cotton is also requisite, and some ufe nothing elfe. The Guilders

com-

commonly border their Cufhion at one end, and four or five inches down each fide, with a ftrip of parchment two inches high, intending by this fence and bulwark to preferve their Gold from the affaults of Wind, and Air, which if moved never fo gently, carries away this light body, which willingly complies with its uncertain motions. Experienced Artifts frequently fhake a whole book of Gold into this end of their Cufhion at one time, and with their knife fingle out the Leaves carefully, and either fpread them whole on their work, or divide and cut 'em, as the bignefs of the place requires : but I would not advife young beginners to prefume fo far, as to operate this way, but venture upon a leaf or two at once, cutting it as above directed. Next, handle your Pencil or Cotton, breathing on it, with which touch and take up the gold ; lay it on the place you defigned it for, prefling it clofe with the faid Pencil or Cotton. Thus proceed, until the whole be finifhed and overlaid ; then cut fome leaves into fmall pieces, which may cover feveral parts of the Frame that have efcaped guilding. Having laid it afide for a day, call for a large fine hogs-hair-brufh ; with this jobb and beat over the work gently, that the gold may be preffed clofe, and compelled to retire into all the uneven, hollow parts of the Carving: Afterwards brufh all the Leaf-gold into a fheet of paper for fale. Laftly, with fine foft, Shammy leather , as it were polifh, and pafs it over. Thefe Rules being ftrictly obferved, your undertaking will be artificially concluded ; 'twill appear with a dazling and unufual luftre, and its beauty will be fo durable, fo well fortified againft the injuries of wind and weather , that the attempts of many Ages will not be able to deface it.

To Lacker in Oyl, fuch things as are to be expofed to the Weather.

In this I requeft you to obferve the very method prefcribed before for guilding, with this difference, That your Primer be more white than the laft, which is effected by mixing a little White-lead, that has been grinded a long time, amongft the former Gold-fize ; farther confidering, that your Silver-fize ought not to be fo dric as that of Gold, when the leaves are to be laid on. Thefe two remarks being rightly obferved, go on with your defign in every particular as aforefaid, and you cannot poffibly mifcarry.

To prepare and guild Carved Frames in Oyl, that are not to be expofed abroad.

Provide a pipkin, in it warm fome Size pretty hot ; bruife with your hand, and put in as much Whiting as will only make it of the fame white colour. Size over your Frame once with it, then add more Whiting, until tis of a reafonable confiftence and thicknefs : With this lay it over three or four times, as you find it deferves, granting it time to drie fufficiently between every turn. Now take a fine Fifh-skin or Dutch-rufhes, and fmooth your Frame with
'em ;

'em; when fo done, you may with a rag, or finger dipt in water, fmooth, or, which is the fame thing in other words, water-plain it to your mind; let it drie. After this, with a fmall quantity of ftrong Size, Cold-clear it; which is a term and name Artifts make ufe of in this cafe to exprefs themfelves by, but is no more then if I had faid in fhort, Size it over: when this is dried, Lacker over your piece by a gentle heat two feveral times. To conclude, lay on your Gold-fize, and perform every thing required in the foregoing inftructions.

CHAP. XIX.

To overlay Wood with burnifht Gold and Silver.

IN order to this work Parchment-fize muft be provided, which is made thus. Take two pounds of the cuttings or fhavings of clean Parchment; the Scriveners vend it for 3d. the pound: wafh and put it into a gallon of fair water, boil it to a Jelly, then ftrain, and fuffer it to cool, and you will find it a ftrong Size. This may be ufed in white Japan alfo, inftead of Ifing-glafs-fize. When you intend to imploy any part of it about the bufinefs in hand, put a proportionable quantity into an earthen pipkin, make it very hot, remove it then from the fire, and fcrape into it as much Whiting as may only colour it; mingle, and incorporate them well together with a clean Brufh. With this whiten your Frame, jobbing and ftriking your Brufh againft it, that the Whiting may enter into every private corner and hollownefs of its carved work; give it reft and leifure to dry. Melt Size again, and put in as much Whiting now as will render it in fome degree thick; with it whiten over your Frame feven or eight times, or as you think beft, ftriking your pencil as aforefaid; never forgetting this caution, to grant a through-drying time between every turn by the fire or Sun: but after the laft, before tis quite dry, dip a clean brufh in water, wet and fmooth it over gently, and rufh it fmooth when dry if you find it neceffary. In the next place, with an inftrument called a Gouge, no broader than a ftraw, open the veins of the Carved work, which your Whiting has choakt and ftopt up. Laftly, procure a fine rag wetted, with which and your finger gently with care fmooth and water-plain it all over; and when tis dry, tis in a capacity to receive your gold-fize; of which in the following Paragraph.

Of Gold and Silver-fize for Burnifhing.

Gold-fize is the chief ingredient that is concerned in this fort of guilding, and tis a difficult task to find the true quantity of each diftinct thing that is required to make up the compofition; and the reafon of it is this, becaufe you are compelled to vary and alter the proportions, as each feafon changes its qualities of moifture and dryth ; for the Summer demands a ftronger Size than the Winter. The moft experienced are uncertain, when they make the Size , whether 'twill anfwer their intentions, and fuffer them to burnifh on it ; therefore to know infallibly how 'twill endure, they lay fome of it on the corner of a Frame, and cover it with Gold or Silver ; now if it does not burnifh well, but is rough, and inclined to fcratch ; add more greafe or oyl, yet avoid too large a quantity. And feeing tis no eafie matter to hit right, and nick the due required mixture, I fhall lay down feveral ways to make it, which I have not only experienced my felf, but are now practifed by fome of the chief Profeffors of it in London.

The beft way to make Silver-fize

Get in readinefs fine Tobacco-pipe-clay , grind it very fmall ; if you pleafe, mix as much Lamblack as will turn it of a light afh-colour ; add to thefe a fmall bit of candle-greafe, grind 'em together extraordinarily fine, granting a mixture of fize and water ; then try it as before directed.

The beft Gold-fize now in ufe.

Take of the beft Englifh and French Armoniack an equal quantity, grind them very finely on a Marble with water, then fcrape into it a little candle-greafe , incorporate and grind all well together.   Again, mix a fmall quantity of parchment-fize with a double proportion of water, and tis all concluded.

Another Size for Silver.

Provide fine Tobacco-pipe-clay, grind a little black lead with it, caft in fome Caftile-foap, grind all of them together , mixing them with a weak Size, as we taught you in the laft account of making Silver-fize.

A Size for Gold or Silver.

Take two drams of Sallet-oyl, one dram of white wax, put 'em into a clean gallipot, only diffolve them on the fire ; to thefe, two drams of black Lead, and near a pound of Bole Armoniack, grind all very finely together, mixing with them alfo fize and water. Remember that I defire you never to grind more gold or filver-fize, than will ferve your prefent neceffities ; if you tranfgrefs, and imagin 'twill be ufeful another time, believe me you'l be deceived when you come to make tryal · more ample and full directions experience will dictate to you , what follows, may be advantageous and inftructive in the preparation of your work.   In order to gold-fize it, If the fubject you are to work on be a carved Frame, and you propofe guilding it, take yellow Oaker, grind it finely with water, add a little weak Size to bind it ; when warm'd, colour over your Frame, pafs by no part of it, permit it to dry leifurely.

To

To Gold-fize your Frame.

Employ either of the former Gold-fizes, yet I am rather inclined to the firſt; melt it, ſo that it be only blood-warm, lay it well with a fine bruſh; as for its condition, let it be ſomewhat thin. With this, ſize over the Frame twice, but touch not the hollow places or deepeſt parts of the Carving, where you cannot conveniently lay your Gold, for the yellow colour firſt laid on is nearer in colour to the gold, ſo that if in guilding you miſs any, the fault will not ſo ſoon be diſcovered. Allow it a drying ſpace of four or five hours, and try if the gold will burniſh on it : if not, alter your gold-ſize, and do it over again, and when dry, thus cover it with.

To lay on Gold for Burniſhing

Having ſet your Frame on an Haſel, or ſixt it in ſome other place, in an upright poſture that the water may run off, and not ſettle in any of the hollowneſſes, lay ſome leaves of Gold on your Cuſhion, which you are to hold in your left hand, with the Pallet and Pencil : alſo tis convenient to have a baſon of water at your feet ; as likewiſe dry Whiting, to rub your knife with ſome times, that the gold may not cling to it. All theſe being advantageouſly placed, and in readineſs, advance forward, and after this manner ſet upon the work. Produce then a Swans-quill-pencil, or a larger tool of Camels-hair if the work require it : this being dipt in water, wet ſo much of your Frame as will take up three or four leaves, beginning at the lower end, aſcending and guilding upwards, laying on whole leaves, or half, as your work calls for them, for your own intereſt contriving how you may beſtow 'em without waſte, which is the principal concernment a Guilder ought to be vigilant and circumſpect in ; and that darling-metal, which we fooliſh Mortals covet, nay almoſt adore, is certainly too precious to be laviſhly conſumed, and unprofitably puff'd away. Then wet ſuch another part of your work, and lay on your gold, with your Pencil or Cotton preſſing it gently and cloſe. By theſe regular ſteps and motions having guilded the two upright ſides of your Frame, turn it, and proceed to operate after the ſame manner by the remaining upper and under part. If your work be ſufficiently moiſt, you'l perceive how lovingly the gold will embrace it, hugging and clinging to it, like thoſe inſeparable friends, Iron and the Loadſtone. I enjoyn you, after the guilding of one ſide with whole, or half leaves, or large pieces, as your work requires, to make a ſtrict enquiry, and review thoſe many little ſpots and places, which, like ſo many Errata, have eſcaped the Pencil, and may thus be regulated : Cut ſome leaves of gold into ſmall pieces, and with a ſmaller pencil than before wet the unguilded parts, and take up bits of gold proportion'd to the places that ſtand in need of it ; this laſt performance we call, Faulting. All theſe things being done, let it ſtand till to morrow that time, and no longer, for if you tranfgrefs, efpecially in the Summer, you'l find it will not burnifh kindly, or recompenfe your trouble by giving you ample fatisfaction.

To Burnifh your Work.

A dog's tooth was formerly lookt upon as the fitteft inftrument for this bufinefs; but of late Aggats and Pebbles are more highly efteemed, being formed into the fame fhapes, for they not only have a fine grain and greet, which conduces to, and heightens the luftre of the gold, but befides it makes a quicker difpatch, for by thefe means thofe narrow tedious ftroaks are prevented in this burnifhing, and is performed with greater expedition. Thefe Pebbles are each valued at 5s. I do therefore prefer and recommend 'em before dogs-teeth. Having burnifht fo much of your work as you defign, leave the ground of your Carving untoucht, and fome other parts as you think beft, which being rough in refpect of the other, fets off and beautifies the burnifhing: that which is not burnifht, muft be matted or fecured with Size, Seed-Lac-varnifh, or Lacker, if you defire it deep-colour'd; and pray confine it to this part only, let not your unfteddy hand wander or tranfgrefs its bounds, and upon no account approach the burnifhing. Then the work muft be fet off or repoffed with Lacker, mixt in a gallipot with Dragons-blood and Saffron, or a colour called, Ornator; into which a fine pencil being dipt, with it touch the hollowneffes of your Carving, the hollow veins of the leaves and foldage, if you imagin tis not deep enough, make it fo by a repetition; fome I know ufe Vermilion in Size, but I declare I am not reconciled to it, for tis not fo pleafant and agreeable to the eye.

To lay on Silver-fize.

Take Silver-fize that's newly ground and mixt with weak Size; warm it as your Gold-fize was, and with a clean pencil, of a bignefs fuitable to the work, fize over the fame once or twice. Let it drie, and if your Silver will burnifh on it, tis fufficient; but on the contrary, if it will not, we advife you to an alteration. Next, wet your work, lay on your Leaf-filver after the method for Gold directly, without any alteration, and burnifh it all over.

Now before we part with this fubject, I fhall in brief lay down a few Rules to be obferved by all Practitioners. And

1. Let your Parchment-fize be fomewhat ftrong, and keep it no confiderable time by you; for 'twill not then be ferviceable.

2. Grind no more Gold or Silver-fize, than what may fupply your prefent neceffities.

3 Preferve your work clean and free from duft, before and after tis gold-fized, and guilded, otherwife twill be full of fcratches in burnifhing.

Laftly, never attempt to whiten, gold-fize, or burnifh it, in the time of a hard froft; for your Whiting will be apt to peel off, the

Gold

Gold and Silver-fize will freez in laying on, not to fay any thing of other misfortunes that attend the unfeafonable operation.

CHAP. XX.

To make good Pafte, fit to mould or raife Carved work on Frames for Guilding.

I Acknowledge this to be utterly ufelefs, on fuppofition thofe perfons who want Frames lived at London, or had any conve nient commerce with, and conveyance from, that City ; becaufe Carved work is there done very cheap and well : but I confult the wants of thofe who cannot be fupplied from thence, or any other place where Artifts refide, who may afford 'em at reafonable rates. In this ftrait and exigency , therefore carve your Frames your felf, after this method. If you underftand Modelling, or defire to make Models on which your Moulds fhall be caft ; take good, tough, well tempered Clay, and with your tools model and work out any fort of Carving which you fancie : lay it afide to drie in the fhade, for either fire or Sun will crack it. When tis firmly dry and hard, and you intend to caft the Moulds on the Models, oyl your models over with Linfeed oyl ; work the pafte briskly be tween your hands, clap it on, and prefs it down clofe every where, that it may be a perfect mould in every part ; and tis no fooner dried, than finifhed.

To make Pafte.

Steep as much glew in water as will ferve you at prefent, then boil it in the faid liquor ; make it ftronger than any fize, yet fome thing weaker than common melted glew : bruife and mix whiting very well with it, until tis as thick and confiftent as pafte or dough; knead it very ftifly, wrapping it up in a double cloath , in which it may lie and receive fome heat from the fire ; if you permit it to lie in the cold and harden, twill render it unferviceable.

To make a Mould of any Carved Frame, thereby to imitate it in Pafte.

Take a piece of pafte more or lefs according to the length or largenefs of the leaves and flowers you take off ; twould be idle and fruitlefs to take off the whole length, for you'l find one bunch of flowers, perhaps fix or eight times in one fide of a frame ; fo that one mould may ferve all of that fort, provided they are artificially united and joined together. Work then the pafte between your hands, clap it on that part of the frame which you defign to take a mould off ; let there be pafte enough, that the back of the mould may be flat and even. While the mould is warm take it from the frame, and at the fame inftant with a weak glew fix it to a board that is larger than it felf. Thus may you take off any other fmall

R   fort

fort of Carving, not only from the infide and edge, but any part of your frame, glewing all your moulds on little boards, and giving them leifure to drie and harden.

Of placing Pafte or Carved work on Frames.

Every Joyner can make frames for this purpofe, which fometimes are very plain mouldings, either half round, ojee or flat ; for there may be fome little hollownefs and ojee, or what elfe you pleafe, allowed of, on the fides of the pafte-work. When your frames, pafte, and moulds are ready, oyl the moulds very well with Linfeed-oyl, ftriking the brufh into every little corner, for this prevents the moulds fticking to the pafte. Then ufe as much warm pafte as will fill up the mould, work it again between your hands, and whilft it is thus warm, and in good temper, put it into the mould, preffing all parts with your thumbs ; next, with a knife cut off the fuperfluous pafte even with the top of the mould : turn out your newly fafhion'd carved work on your hand, and before it cools glew it, and the place tis defign'd for, with thin glew ; clap it on your work in the very place you intend it fhall always abide, preffing it gently. Then oyl your mould again, work your pafte, caft and place it as before this muft be repeated, until the whole be accomplifhed, and the frame is to your content filled with carving. Grant it four or five days to dry in, after which time you may fafely whiten it. On thefe forts of frames you may guild in oyl, or burnifh, but to the latter it is chiefly accommodated.

CHAP. XXI.

Of Lackering.

LAckers are compofed feveral ways, and differ as varioufly in their value and goodnefs, which admits of degrees, according to the method and materials out of which they are produced ; yet they have common to them all in which they univerfally agree, the famous ingredients, Spirit of Wine, and Seed or Lac-fhell-varnifh ; but their Colour and Tincture for all this differ extreamly. Some boil their Lacker, whilft others (who are more in the right) are not beholding either to Fire or Sun. They who through ignorance diffolve it by fire, are in the firft place to be excufed, as alfo when they cannot rife to the price of good Spirits, ftrong enough to diffolve the Seed or Shell-lacc without fire ; but becaufe fome may be willing to fave charges, and others defire indifferent Lacker only, take along with you directions for them both.

TO

To make common Lacker.

Take one quart of Spirit, put it into a Pottle-bottle; of Shell-Lacc eight ounces, beaten fmall enough to enter the bottle; fhake 'em well together; having ftood till quite diffolved, ftrain it, and reduce to powder a fmall quantity of Sanguis Draconis, which with a little Turmerick tied up in a rag put into it, grant it a days continuance in that pofture, at your leifure hours fhaking it. You may alter the colour, heighten or abate it, by adding or diminifhing the quantity of the two latter ingredients.

Another fort of Lacker.

Ufe the fame quantity of Spirit of Wine and Shell-Lacc as before; when diffolved, ftrain it; but, to give it a tincture, inftead of common Dragons-blood and Turmerick, employ a very little Sanguis Draconis in drops, and Saffron dried; which bruife, and cloath with a piece of linnen, and manage it as the other, by putting it into the veffel. If you defire the Lacker of a deeper or more copperifh colour, add more Sanguis; if the contrary, Saffron. Thefe being fhakt well, keep clofe ftopt for your defigns.

To make the beft fort of Lacker now ufed by the Guilders.

Some ufe Shell-lacc-varnifh only for this Lacker, but Seed-lacc is much better, the compofition of which you are taught in the 8th page. Take therefore of this feed-lacc-varnifh, a quantity anfwerable to the Lacker, which give a tincture to after this manner. Take the colour called Ornator, ground and reduced to a very fine dry powder; mix it and fome of the varnifh in a gallipot, ftir and diffolve it over a gentle fire; after this confine 'em to a viol clofely ftopt. Take likewife three or four ounces of Gambogium, which I would have bruifed, diffolved on the fire, and kept in a vial as the other. To a quart of this varnifh, if you pleafe, two penniworth of Saffron dried and bruifed may be added; to thefe, five or fix fpoonfuls of the Ornator, and a double portion of Gambogium-varnifh. being fhaked well together, try it on a little bit of filver, or a fmall frame; if it appears too yellow, afford more from your Ornator, but if too red, from your Gambogium vial: by thefe contrivances you may continue the mixture until you arrive at the true golden colour, which is the only excellence we defign and aim at.

To make a Lacker, that may be ufed without Fire or Sun.

To a quart of the aforefaid Lacker allow 2 penniworth of Venice Turpentine; mix and incorporate them very well. With this you may lacker any thing in the open Air, and although it may

look

' ... and and mifty immediately after every lackering, that fright,
a feeming difcouragement, will quickly vanifh ; that thin clou-
dy vapour, will be diffipated by its fudden, and piercing luftre.

To lacker Oyl, Size, or Burnifht Silver.

Let your Frame or work be warmed before you lacker it, and
when fome of your Lacker is poured into a large Gallipot, with a
fine large Brufh, that does not drop any of its hairs, made of Hogs
or Camels-hair, be quick and pafs over the piece, carefully contriving to mifs no part, or to repafs another that has been already lac-
kered ; but in a manner obferve the fame rules here, that are given
for Japan, yet with thefe exceptions in lackering Carved work ;
for then you muft be quick, and ftrike or jobb your brufh, thereby
to cover the deep parts alfo : Be fure to lay it thin and even, and
prefently warm it by the fire whilft it looks bright, for by thefe
means you may lacker it again in a quarter of an hour, warming it
before and after the operation. If two or three varnifhings will
not produce a colour deep enough, oblige it with a fourth ; but remember, if you fhould carelefly do it too deep, all affiftance will be
infignificant, and no remedy whatfoever will avail you.

To make Lackering fhew like Burnifht Gold.

If you are careful and neat in burnifhing your filver, and have
graced your Lacker with a true gold-colour, have with an even
hand laid it no thicker in one place than another ; then Matt and
Repoffe it, as you do burnifht gold ; and unlefs narrowly furveyed,
twill put a fallacy upon and deceive curious, difcerning eyes. Mat-
ting is only the ground-work of your Carving altered, or varnifhing it deeper and more dull than the other part of the Frame : Re-
poffing is done with Lacker and Ornator, (which latter the Drug-
fters fell at 4d the ounce,) with thefe mixt, touch and deepen all
the hollow deep places and veins of your work ; for it adorns and
fets it off admirably well, by ite colour and reflection.

CHAP. XXII.

Of Guilding Metals.

I Acquainted you before with a controverfy between the Guilders, concerning the Terms of Art, who denied the name of
Guilding to that of Wood, and confined it to Metals only : upon
which account we promifed you to treat of the latter too, and thereby comprehend both ; although tis no queftion but one laics as juft
a claim to that title as the other. They are certainly fine inventions, that ferve to pleafe us with the fhadow , when the fubftance
can-

can't be purchafed. We are all of us great admirers of Gold, and by confequence muft be enamoured with Guilding, which is fo nearly related to it. For Guilding is Gold in Miniature,with which as with a golden Ray, we beautify and adorn our viler Metals. Its preparation therefore muft firft be difcovered, before we can proceed to the ufe and performance.

To prepare Gold.

Take Leaf, or fine Ducket-gold, which is more excellent for this ufe, of either what quantity you pleafe ; but be fure that the Ducket be beaten very thin : put the gold, and as much quick-filver as will juft cover it, into a gallipot. Let them ftand half an hour, prefently after the mixture ftirring them with a ftick. This time being expired, ftrain 'em through a piece of leather, fqueezing with your hand, till you have brought out as much quick-filver as will be fore t through by all your induftry. Now that which remains in the leather looks more like filver than gold, yet tis that, and that alone which muft be employed in the fucceeding operation

To guild Silver, Copper, Brafs, or Princes-metal.

Whatfoever you defign for guilding, fhould be firft well ferubbed with a Wier-brufh, fold by the Iron-mongers. Wet the piece with water or beer, and continue ferubbing and wetting it, until all filth and dirtinefs be fetcht off, that the two metals may more clofely hug and embrace each other. This being cleans'd, make ready quick-filver, by mixing it with a very fmall quantity of Aqua fortis in a vial, which fhould always ftand by you ; three or four drops only of Aqua fortis, is fufficient I affure you for an ounce of quick-filver. With this quicken your work, that is, with your finger or a fine rag rub this mixture on your metal, till tis all over-filvered or toucht with the faid quick-filver. This done, call for your gold formerly prepared, and with an iron-tool or little knife fit for the purpofe, fpread or overlay the whole work, being careful to mifs no part, under the penalty of doing that place over again, after you have given it an heat over a fire , which you muft do when the gold is laid, to compel the Mercury or quick-filver to evaporate and flie away, leaving the gold fixed and adhering clofe to the piece. But before you give it a through heat, let it have two or three little heats, that you may with a hair-brufh, like that of a comb, dab and fpread your gold, which by the little warmth you gave it, makes the quickfilver alfo more ready to fpread. After thefe two or three vifits made to the fire, give it the thorough-heat at firft mentioned : then take it from the fire, and with a ferub-brufh, that has never been toucht with quickfilver, clean it, as you did in the beginning. Now, if you perceive any fpot of quickfilver untoucht, you muft lay your gold upon it again: when tis cleaned with the fcratch-brufh, you may after this manner heighten its colour, if you think convenient.

S   Take

Take of Salt, Argal, and Brimſtone, an equal quantity; mix them with as much fair water as will cover the thing when put in-to it ; boil them over the fire, and having tied your guilded work to a ſtring, put it into the boiling liquor for a little ſpace, looking on it every minute, and when it has acquired a colour that pleaſes you, dip it in cold water, and the whole is finiſhed. But ſtill if you would have the work more rich and laſting, you may again quicken it with quickſilver and aqua fortis, and guild it over again after the former method, and repeat it ſo often, if you pleaſe, till your gold lies as thick as your nail upon the metal.

Another way to guild Silver, Braſs, or Princes-metal.

Firſt, bruſh over your ſilver with Aqua fortis, then quicken your work with Mercury as before taught. Let your gold be beaten thin, and put into a Crucible, with juſt ſo much quickſilver as will cover it, and let it ſtand till it begin to blubber: then ſtrain it through a piece of leather as before, and the quickſilver will go through and leave your gold, but diſcoloured, as hath been ſaid ; then lay it on with an iron-tool, and in every thing do as you were taught in the other guilding.

Another way to heal, or heighten, the Colour of your Gold.

Take Sal Armoniack, Salt-petre , Sandiver, Verdigreece, white and green Vitriol, grind them with white-wine vinegar, which lay all over your work; then lay it on a fire, and give it a ſmall heat that may make it ſmoak, and then take it off and quench it in urine.

To take off Gold from any guilt Plate, without the damage of one, or loſs of the other.

Put as much Sal Armoniack, finely beaten, into Aqua fortis, as will make it thick like a Paſte ; ſpread your Plate all over with it, put it into the fire, give it a thorough heat, neal it, or make it red hot ; then quench it in fair water, and with a ſcrub-bruſh ſcratch and ſcrub the Plate very well, which will fetch off all the gold into the water. After a little time ſtanding quietly, pour off your wa-ter, and the gold will be to your ſatisfaction found at the bottom ; if all the gold be not come off, do the ſame again. As for cleanſing this plate, or any other, which we call, Boiling of ſilver, firſt, make your plate red hot, let it ſtand till tis cold; then mix Argal and Salt with water, when it boils , put in your plate, keeping it there for a quarter of an hour: take it out, and when waſhed and rinſed in fair water, you'l perceive by its beauty that tis ſufficiently changed.

To Silver-over Braſs or Copper, as the Clockmakers do their Dial-plates.

Having Leaf or burnt-ſilver in readineſs, put it into as much Aqua fortis as will cover it; after an hours ſtanding pour off the Aqua fortis as clean as may be from the ſilver; waſh the ſilver
three

three or four times with water, let it dry, and then mix it with
one part of fine Argal to three of silver, with a little fair water.
When you make ufe of it, rub it on the work with a cork, until tis
all filvered, and lie as fair as you could wifh. Next, dry it well
with a linnen cloth, and having made it warm, wafh it over three
or four times with the beft white varnifh, fpoken of in this book,
and it will not fail to fecure it from Tarnifhing, and other injuries.

To guild Iron, Brafs, or Steel, with Leaf-gold or Silver.

If you are to guild Brafs or old Iron, you muft cleanfe it very
well with a Scratch-brufh, before you hatch or guild on it ; but
for new Iron or Steel, after you have filed it very fmooth, take
a hatching-knife, (which is only a knife with a fhort blade and
long handle,) and hatch your work all over neatly ; then give it an
heat, whilft it looks blew, on a charcoal fire, from whence take it
and lay on your gold or filver, and with a fanguine-ftone burnifh it
down a little ; then give it the fame heat and burnifh it all over.
Thus may you repeat three or four, or half a dozen, or a dozen
times if you pleafe, ftill obferving to give it the fame heat before
and after you lay on your gold or filver, and burnifh it. This leaf-
gold and filver is much thicker than the other, and four times as
dear.

To refine Silver.

Take Silver, be it never fo coarfe, and melt it in a melting-pot,
then caft it into water, to make it hollow ; after tis cold take it
out and dry it, mixing one ounce of Salt-petre to a penni-weight of
Antimony, (fo proportionably greater quantities, if you have occafion.) Thefe with your Silver confine again to a melting-pot, covering that with another, very clofely luting them together with
loam, made of clay and horfe-dung. The two pots being thus ce-
mented, put 'em into the fire, and give them a very ftrong heat,
after which remove them to a cooling place. Break the pot when
cold, and you'l perceive the filver fine at the bottom, but the
fcorio and drofs on the upper part like a cinder. Copper may be
feparated from Gold after the fame manner.

To feparate Gold and Silver, when incorporated, with Aqua fortis.

Take as much Aqua fortis duplex, as will fomething more than
cover your metal, in a ftrong vial or parting-glafs. Put it on
fand over a gentle fire at firft, with the glafs open and unftopt ;
for if tis clofed twill break in pieces, as may alfo a fierce fire at the
beginning : by degrees therefore increafe its heat, till you make
the Aqua fortis fimper and boil ; continue fo doing, till your metal be diffolved. This done, pour the Aqua fortis gently into water ; the filver will invifibly go along with it, but the gold remain
at the bottom of the glafs ; which gold, when well wafhed with

water, you may melt down, or preserve for guilding metals, by mixing it with quickfilver, and ftraining the latter through leather, as you were inftructed by Leaf and Ducket-gold.

Now to reduce the filver into its former body which appears to be a water, and fo would remain many years, unlefs you take this method for its alteration ; pour the faid water (wherein your filver is floating like undifcernable Atoms) into a copper veffel , if in any other, put in copper-plates ; and immediately all the filver will repair to the copper, like an army to their pofts at beat of drum, fo that in two or three hours time (that fmall parcel of filver, which hath been feparated into parts more innumerable than the Turks army will be this Campagne) you'l find all hanging and clinging fo lovingly to the copper, and as loth to part as we from our Miftreffes, tho they're fometimes more unconftant to us than the filver is to the copper, for no other metal can tempt it to the fame compliance. The fame filver fo gathered you may ufe for filvering any metal, doing with it as is here taught of the gold, or inftead of leaf or burnt filver diffolved in Aqua fortis, as was before faid in Clockmakers filvering.

CHAP.

Directions in Painting MEZZOTINTO - Prints,
on *Glaſs, or without it.*

CHAP. XXIII.

THis moſt ingenious way of Painting juſtly claims applauſe and admiration, if skill and dexterity are called to the performance · Where theſe two combine, beauty and perfection muſt dance attendance. Tis a pleaſant, inſinuating Art ; which, under a pretty diſguiſe betrays us into a miſtake : We think a piece of Limning lies before us, bur more ſtrict enquiries will evince, that tis Mezzo-tinto at the bottom; Who can be diſpleaſed to be ſo innocently deluded, and enamoured at the ſame time ? Tis female policy at once to raviſh and deceive the eyes, and we not only careſs the cheat, but are in love with the impoſtor too. This manner of Painting is lookt upon to be the Womens more peculiar province, and the Ladies are almoſt the only pretenders ; yet with modeſty and ſubmiſſion I may adventure to affirm, that I have not had the good fortune to meet with one of an hundred, that had an excellent command of the Pencil, or could deſervedly be ſtiled a Miſtreſs of this Art ; yet tis certainly no uneaſie task to arrive to a great height in it : but we are overſtockt with no leſs conceited than ignorant Teachers, well qualified to deface a Print, and ſpoil the colours, who abuſe thoſe young Ladies that deſire inſtructions, perſwading 'em to the damage of their purſes, and loſs of their time to attempt that which they are not able ſo much as to aſſiſt 'em in. This is a ſufficient inducement to perſwade my ſelf, that theſe Rules will be acceptable ; tho I know very well that I have raiſed a diſcourſe on a ſubject with which the world is very well acquainted, yet by way of requital I ſhall make greater diſcoveries than the famous Miſtreſs of it ever pretended to communicate ; in a word, I promiſe to diſplay it in its perfection.

I conceive tis requiſite to adviſe you, firſt, in the election of Prints, Frames, and Glaſs ; of each in their order. Mezzo-tinto Prints are to be preferred before all others , being more fit and ſuitable for Painting than thoſe that are engraved, for in theſe all the ſtroaks of the Graver are plainly viſible ; but the other, if done with a near and careful hand, on a good, fine-grounded print, can hardly be diſtinguiſht from Limning. Conſider, that ſome of theſe Prints are of a coarſe ground, others of a fine : the firſt are diſcernible, for they ſeem to be rough, and workt as it were with the pricks of a Pen ; but the latter hath ſoft and fine ſhadows, like a piece neatly wrought in Indian ink, or a picture in black and white.

T   Ob-

Obferve farther what paper they are drawn upon ; for if it be too thick, which you may forefee by wetting a corner of it with water or your tongue, and it pafs not through the paper prefently, then conclude tis not for your purpofe ; but on the contrary, the thin and fpungy paper muft be elected : Their value is enhanced by the different fize and goodnefs of each Print ; fome may be afforded for fix pence or a fhilling, others for 18d. or more.

Your Glafs ought to be thin, white, and well polifht, fuch as is made for Looking-glafies. All blewifh, red, green, and window-glafs, cannot be allowed of here, you muft altogether defpife and cafhier it ; for if you paint on either of thefe, efpecially window-glafs, your colours can never appear fair and beautiful.

Your Frames for glafs-painting are ufually made of ftained Pear-tree, with narrow mouldings for little pieces, which increafe in bredth, as the fize of your picture does in largenefs ; they are made with Rabets, and are afforded for 6,8, and 12 pence, or more, according to their feveral dimenfions.

Another fort of Frames I recommend to you, moft proper for thofe Prints which you paint without glafs, called Straining-frames : If you defire to have them Carved, Guilded, or black, order them to be made flat, and even, without a Rabet on the back-fide, half an inch lefs than the edge of the Cutt, every way ; which is apt to rend when it undergoes the trial of ftraining. This mif-chance is occafioned by the fharp edge of the Plate, which almoft cuts the paper when tis printed : If you approve of black Frames, command the Frame-maker to work them half round with Pear-tree ; would you ftain, or Japan them, guild or raife their carved work ; this Book will fufficiently inform and direct you. Thus much of thefe things in particular ; I fhall now proceed to give a catalogue of fuch Colours as may be affiftant to you in this bufi-nefs, together with the Oyls, and their feveral prices ; as alfo dire-ctions to make drying Oyl, and various forts of Varnifh for Paint-ing. And firft, the names of your colours, and their value, as they are commonly fold ready prepared, take in the very order that they are placed on your Pallet.

Flake White, finely ground in Nut-oyl, is fold at 2s. the pound. White-lead, ground in the fame oyl, 1s. per pound.

Yellow and brown Oaker, finely ground in Linfeed oyl, is vended for 3d. the ounce.

Yellow or Dutch Pink may be afforded, when ground, at the fame rate.

Brown or glafing-Pink is indeed very dear, the bignefs of a Nut-meg grinded will ftand you in 6d.

Fine Lake will coft as much.

Light and brown Red, are only yellow and brown Oaker burnt ; tis 3d. the ounce ready ground.

Italian Terravert, is not much ufed in this Painting, though very much in all others ; tis dearer fometimes than at others.

Umber

Umber, Collins-Earth, Ivory, blew black, are afforded at the ordinary price when ground, which is 3d. the ounce.

Diftilled Verdegreas ground, you may have at the fame rate with Brown Pink and Lake; but thefe three colours I would advife you to purchafe by the Ounce, and grind 'em your felf, if it will ftand with your conveniency; for the Colour-Grocers will afford thefe cheaper by the Ounce than Dram. Its price is 1s. the Ounce; indifferent brown Pink, and Lake, for the fame value: but that which is more pure and fine, is 1s. 6d. 2s. and 2s. 6d. or more, as they excell in goodnefs.

Some Colours are in powder, which you muft of neceflity have by you, and fhould mix and temper on your Pallet, as you fhall have occafion to ufe them.

The firft is Vermilion, ufually fold at 4d. the Ounce.

Carramine, being the fineft and moft excellent Red, is fometimes vended for 3l. the Ounce.

For Blews, the beft fine Smalt is to be bought for 4 or 5s. the pound.

Blew Bice, ufeful only in making green colours, may be gotten for 4d. or 6d. an Ounce.

Ultramarine, the richeft blew in the world, bears feveral prices. the deepeft and beft will coft 6 or 7 Guinea's, but then it muft be extraordinary fine; other forts are expofed for 3 or 4l. the Ounce, which is very good too, and fit for this ufe; fome again for 20s. the fame quantity, and may ferve for Painting, but tis too coarfe for glazing.

Yellow and pale Mafticott, which is fineft, free from greet, with the brighteft colour, is the beft. If it prove coarfe, grind or wafh it a little on a clean ftone; tis fold for 2d. the Ounce.

Red Orpiment you muft mix with drying Oyl; this too is afforded for 2d. the Ounce.

Thefe are the Colours ufeful in Painting, with which you may exactly imitate and hit any colour whatfoever, by different ways and methods of mixture. Their price alfo I have given you, if you buy them in fmall parcels; but if you furnifh your felf with greater quantities at one time, you'l find the purchafe more cheap, and eafie. Obferve, that fix of thefe are tranfparent or glazing colours, viz. Brown Pink, fine Lake, Carramine, fine Smalt, Ultramarine, and Diftilled Verdegreas.

To wafh, or make any of the Powders very fine.

You muft have four or five large Wine-glaffes by you, and two or three quarts of clear water. Fill one of your glaffes with it, put in half an Ounce, or as much of your colour as you intend to wafh; ftir it well about with your knife, permit it to ftand no longer than while you could count or tell forty; for in this fhort fpace of time all the coarfe will fink and fettle to the bottom, the

finer

finer remains floating in the water, which convey and pour off into another glafs, leaving the coarfe part behind. Let the veffel, with the fine colour and water, ftand till next day, by which time that alfo will fettle to the bottom of the water. This being poured off, take out the colour; place it on a clean fmooth Chalk-ftone, to foak and drink up the water; and when 'tis dry, paper it up for your bufinefs.

Of OYLs.

It remains, that to this account of Colours, we fubjoyn that of Oyls, which muft be ferviceable to us in the Art of Painting.

The firft of thefe is Linfeed Oyl, fold at 8d. the quart.

Nut-Oyl, to be purchafed at 16 or 18d. the like quantity.

Oyl of Turpentine is afforded for lefs than 8d. the pound.

Drying-Oyl, will ftand you in 2d. an Ounce at the Colour-fhops, and Fine-varnifh 3d. which in my opinion is too dear; and therefore, if you'l give your felf the trouble, I'le be at the pains to inftruct you, how to make either fort.

To make the beft Drying-Oyl.

Mix a little Letharge of Gold with Linfeed-Oyl, for a quarter of an hour boil it; if you'd have it ftronger, continue boiling it, but not too much neither, left it prove over-thick and unferviceable.

Another more ordinary.

Bruife Umber and Red-lead to powder, mix 'em with Linfeed-oyl, and for boiling follow the directions foregoing. When this Oyl has ftood a day or two, and you find a skin over it, know then for certain 'tis at your fervice.

To make Varnifhes for thefe Prints, or Pictures in oyl.

Put an Ounce of Venice-Turpentine into an earthen pot, place it over a fire, and when diffolved and melted thin, add to it two ounces of oyl of Turpentine; as foon as they boil take off the pot, and when the varnifh is cool, keep it in a glafs-bottle. This and all other varnifhes ought to be ftopt clofe, and fecured from the approaches and damage of the Air. With this you may varnifh your Prints on glafs or others, to render them tranfparent; this is what the Shops fell for fine varnifh: fhould your varnifh be too thick, relieve it by an addition of Oyl of Turpentine.

Another more excellent Varnifh either for Pictures in oyl, or making Prints tranfparent.

Inclofe fix ounces of the cleareft, white, well-pickt Maftick finely powdered, in a bottle with fixteen ounces of oyl of Turpentine; ftop and fhake them well together, till they are incorporated. Then hang the bottle in a veffel of water, but not fo deep as to touch the botom; boil the water for half an hour, in which fpace you muft

take

take it out three or four times to fhake it ; if you'd have it ftronger, boil it a quarter of an hour more. I could give you a greater number of Recipe's, but 'twill be too irkfome, tedious, and unneceffary, feeing thefe will preferve your pictures, and are as good in their kind as any Varnifhes whatfoever

---

CHAP. XXIV.

To lay Prints on Glaß.

HAving at large treated of the Colours, Oyls, and other materials required in this work ; I proceed to inftruct you how the Prints themfelves muft be laid on Glafs First therefore let your Prints be fteeped in warm water flat-ways, for four or five hours, or more, if the paper be thick : provide then a thin pliable knife, with it fpread Venice-Turpentine thin and even over the glafs, and with your finger dab and touch it all over, that the Turpentine may appear rough. Next, take the Print out of the water, lay it on a clean Napkin very evenly, and with another prefs every part of it lightly, to fuck and drink up the water of it ; afterwards lay the print on the glafs by degrees, beginning at one end, ftroaking outwards that part which is faftning to the glafs, that between it and the Print no wind or water may lurk and hide it felf, which you muft be careful of, and never fail to ftroke out. Then wet the backfide of the print, and with a bit of fpunge or your finger rub it over lightly, and the paper will role off by degrees ; but be careful, and avoid rubbing holes, efpecially in the lights, which are moft tender : and when you have peeled it fo long, that the Print appears tranfparent on the backfide, let it dry for two hours ; next, varnifh it over with Maftick or Turpentine-varnifh four or five times, or fo often, till you may clearly fee through it. After a nights time for drying, you may work on it.

To lay Prints, either graved, or Mezzo-tinto's, in fuch manner, that you may role off all the paper, and leave the fhadow behind.

Soak the Print in water, dry it with a cloath, fpread on the glafs oyl of Maftick: and fome Turpentine, and lay on the print upon it, exactly as before. When tis almoft dry, brufh off the paper with a brufh, and you'l find none but the inky, fhadowed part remain : then do this as the former with Maftick-varnifh, which preferve dry and free from duft, until you are at leifure to paint upon it.

To prepare Prints without glafs or ftraining-frames.

When your prints are fteeped fufficiently in water, lay them on a fmooth, wet Table, with the print-fide downwards, and rub 'em thin as before for glafs. Next, with common pafte, do the backfide of your frame, and pafte on your print while wet give it leifure

V

fure to dry, and then varnish it on both sides four or five times
with Maftick or Turpentine-varnish, until tis so transparent, that
you may see the Picture as plain on the back as foresside. Lastly,
allow it a day or two for drying.

I may now very reasonably suppose, that all things are in readiness, and that nothing may hinder us from setting about the work
in earnest. Most Ladies that have practised this Art have
made use of an uneasie posture for themselves, and a disadvantagi-
ous situation for their piece : for they generally stand to it when
the windows are high, against which they place the Print ; but
whosoever stands, cannot so steddily move the hand and pencil as
the person that sits down. I advise you therefore to a Table Ha-
sel, very like to, and not improperly called, a Reading-desk ; only
with this difference, That where the Panel or back-board for the
book is, there our Painting-desk may be all open, with three or
four wiers pendant-wise, to keep the picture from falling through,
and a narrow ledge at the bottom to support it. Beside these, I
would have little holes made equally distant on both sides of the
Desk, as tis remarkable in Painters Hasels, that by pegs or pins,
and a narrow ledge laid upon them, I may raise my Picture higher
or lower, as it best suits with my conveniency. Being thus fixt,
lay a sheet of very white paper behind the picture on the table, and
you'l find it much better, and more conveniently placed than a-
gainst the window.

How to paint a Mezzo-tinto-Landskip on Glass, or otherwise.

The first thing to be attempted in this work, whether Landskip
or others, is Glazing all those places that require it ; and if you
desire they should lie thin, and drie quickly, (as they ought to do,)
mix varnish when you lay them on, and in four hours time they'l
be ready for the reception of other colours. In Landskip, you
should first glaze the nearest and great trees, and ground 'em with
brown Pink, or, if you fancie them greener, add distilled Verdegreas. The trees, that are to appear with a lively, beautiful green,
as also the leaves and weeds, that are in some pictures, must be glazed with Dutch-Pink, and distill'd Verdegreas ; the trees farther
off, with Verdegreas alone ; the hills, mountains, and trees, at the
greatest distance of all, remember to glaze with fine Smalt, a little
Lake, and Verdegreas, all thinly mixt with varnish. As for the
Skie, although several Mistresses practise and teach the cutting of
it out from the picture, and painting it on the glass, I do by no
means allow of it, for it agrees not with the eye, but makes that
part which should seem more distant, appear too nigh and before
the rest ; in a word, it spoils and disparages the whole piece. I cannot suggest to my self any reason for this foolish contrivance, unless

2

a fenfe of their inabilities to paint 'em beautifully, obliges them to commit fo great an abfurdity. Take then Ultramarine, or, for want of that, fine Smalt; mix it thin with varnifh, and glaze it over two or three times with a clean large Pencil, and a very fwift ftroak; for if you're tedious, it will dry fo faft, that you cannot poffibly lay it even. If the Landskip be adorned with Figures, Buildings, Rocks, Ruins, or the like, they require finifhing firft of all. The mixture of colours for thefe things confifts chiefly of white, black, and yellow, fometimes a tincture of red; but the management and compofition of them I leave to your inclination, fancy, and experience yet I would have you confider, that all your Colours for this fort of Painting ought to be extraordinary light. Now to finifh the Trees, Ground, and Sky, and the reft of the picture, begin as before with the greateft or neareft trees, and with yellow Pinke and white, paint over the lighteft leaves; but with a darker colour of Pink, and a little Smalt, do neatly over the darkeft and outward leaves with a fmall pencil dipt in varnifh. Thofe trees you would have beautiful, paint with a mixture of yellow Mafticott, Verdegreas, and white; the darker parts with Pink, Verdegreas, and white; as thofe trees alfo which you glazed with Verdegreas only, they being mixt very light with white. But to finifh the skie and forreskip; if any clouds appear, touch them with varnifh and light colour, made of white, yellow Oaker, and Lake: With thefe likewife touch the lighteft parts of hills, and towns, at the remoteft diftance; then mix Smalt and White as light as you can conveniently, and paint over the skie; add to thefe a tincture of Lake, and do over the darker clouds: Let your colours lie thin, and even; if the whole be finifhed, grant it time to drie in. If you would have your Picture look more ftrong, brisk, and lively, fet it againft the light, or on the Hafel as before; and although 'tis painted all over, you may perceive the fhadows and lights through it; if not, what you painted before will guide you. Paint then your skie and forefight with the fame but lighter colours than before, and fo every thing elfe refpectively.

CHAP. XXV.

To Paint a piece of figures, as Men, Women, &c.

IN painting a Face, the firft thing required is, if there are any deep fhadows, to glaze and touch them thinly with Lake, brown Pink, and Varnifh; alfo the white fpeck and black ball, or fight of the eye, as the Print will direct you; the round white ball of a convenient colour too. If you make the lips of a delicate red, glaze them with Carramine, or Lake: For the reft of the face, begin with the dark fide, and paint the fhadows with a colour more

V 2   red

red than ordinary, for which Vermilion, yellow Pink, and white, are moſt proper; where note, that all varniſh is forbid in painting fleſh-colours, except what is uſed in glazing the ſhadows: if you ſhould mix varniſh, the inconvenience will be, that the colours will drie ſo faſt, that you cannot ſweeten the ſhadows with the fleſh. Then give ſome touches on the ſtrongeſt lights of the face, as the top of the noſe, forehead, and by the eyes, mouth, and chin, with a colour made of white, pale Maſticott, or yellow Oaker, and a little vermilion, and mixed according to the complexion intended; then mix that colour a thought darker, and lay it on all the face, that was not painted before, very carefully; yet for the mouth, and cheeks, ſomewhat redder. Next, with a fine clean pencil, that has been uſed and worn a little, hatch and ſweeten all your fleſh-colours and ſhadows ſweetly together, cleanſing the pencil as often as tis requiſite. Cheeks too pale, or any other part, may be regulated with ſuitable colours, whilſt the piece is moiſt and wet. For ſwarthy complexions, mix the fleſh-colour with white, yellow or brown Oaker, and light red, with ſhadows agreeable. I requeſt you to obſerve the ſame method in painting breaſts, hands, or naked bodies, as for the face: When any of theſe are drie, you may go over them again, by which ſecond painting you may effectually mix your colours to your humor. Laſtly, be ever careful, that your pencil be ſteddily guided, without the leaſt ſlip or treſpaſs upon lines and features of a diſagreeing colour.

To Paint Hair.

Tis not convenient in this Painting to uſe Varniſh or Colours neer ſo dark as the life, for the Print will darken it: as for example; Suppoſe I were to paint an head of hair that is black, I would mix white, black, red Oaker, with a touch of Lake or light red, all which may produce an aſh-colour; and the hair or Peruke being coloured with it, will repreſent a natural black. Now to make the curles ſhew ſtronger, touch the lighteſt parts with a lighter colour, and the darkeſt with the contrary; all which you may ſee through, if they are not laid too thick.

To paint Drapery or Garments.

To paint a piece of Drapery or Cloath, of a broken colour, you muſt take care of its mixture; yet you are to make three degrees of the ſaid colour, that is one, the very colour, another more light, the third darker: this laſt is for the darkeſt folds, the lighteſt for the lighteſt pleats, and the colour between both for the other part of the garment; ſweeten the colour with a worn pencil, that the folds may not lie hard. If you have a mind to embroider a garment, make fringe, or any other parts with ſhell or powdered Gold or Siver, mix then your metals with gum-water, and with a
fine

fine pencil hatch or embroider your flowers, and touch the fringes, or what elfe beft pleafes you, before you either glaze or paint the garment you defign to adorn, after this manner.

How to paint changeable Drapery.

Imagine that your garment to be painted had its ground purple, and the lights yellow; take then a fine pencil dipt in varnifh, and with yellow Mafticott touch thinly all the lighteft parts of your folds; if there be occafion repeat it, for your colour muft be very thin with varnifh: when drie, glaze it all over with Lake and Ultramarine, or Smalt with varnifh once or twice, and let it drie; then mix three degrees of a purple colour, one of Lake, Smalt, and White, and lay them on, as the laft Paragraph directs you.

To paint feveral forts of Red Drapery; and, firft, of the Fineft.

Take Carramine, and mix it thin with varnifh alone; glaze over your garment once, if you'd have it very beautiful, two hours after do the fame again; and when that is drie, with vermilion and white, or vermilion only, you may paint all except the dark fhadows, which fhould have red. If you can fee through the colour when drie, the lighteft folds, touch them over with clear white, and they will appear more rich and ornamental.

Another Red near the fame.

Grind Lake very finely in oyl, temper it well with drying oyl and varnifh; with this glaze over your Drapery two or three times, and when tis dry, paint the lighteft with white, the darkeft with light or brown red, the remainder with vermilion.

Other Reds more ordinary, without Glazing.

Mix vermilion and white, and paint the ftrongeft lights with it; the dark fhadows with a light or dark red, and the reft with vermilion. For the lighteft folds, mix light red and white; for the dark pleats, brown red; for the reft, light red only.

To paint the beft Blew, and glaze with Ultramarine.

Mix Ultramarine with thick Nut-oyl; but if you cannot wait and attend its drying two or three days, then inftead of oyl ufe varnifh, and glaze your garment three or four times over, letting it dry between every turn; when tis dried, make three degrees of Smalt and White very light, and with the cleareft white do the lighteft folds, and the reft as directed in the other colours. If you are unwilling to beftow Ultramarine upon it, you may after the fame method glaze with fine Smalt, and varnifh it as often as with the former, and paint it with White and Smalt: An indifferent Blew is made with White and Smalt, mixt in feveral degrees without glazing.

To glaze and paint the best Purple-Drapery.

Glaze the garments thin, once over with Carramine, or Lake; when tis dry, paint it every where with Smalt and White, lighter or darker as you think best, but let the lightest folds have still a colour more light than the rest. Contrary to this you may produce a purple, by glazing your work over once or twice with Ultramarine, or Smalt, and paint it with Lake and White.

Purple without glazing.

Make a mixture of Lake, Smalt, and White, with which paint the Drapery, heightning and darkening the folds as in the other Receipts.

Yellow Drapery.

For your lightest folds, mingle yellow Oaker, and White; and brown Oaker for the shades: if that is not dark enough, Umber will make it so; but do over the other pleats with yellow Oaker. Such another colour may be made with White, yellow and brown Pink.

To paint the most beautiful Yellow.

Glaze your Drapery, or any thing you would have lovely, with brown Pink once or more, and the darkest parts oftner; after tis dried, touch the lightest folds with pale Masticott, the next with yellow Masticott: if some require a colour darker than that, mix yellow or brown Pink; but for the saddest of all, use yellow Pink and a little Umber. When tis drie, you may paint all with white, except the shades.

To finish, varnish, and polish Pictures, that are not laid upon Glass.

These desire the same proceedings with those on Glass, unless you have a mind to adorn Embroidery, Fringe, or the like, with Gold or Silver. Touch then the forside of your picture with shell-gold in gum-water; or else, after you have varnisht it two or three times with varnish made of Spirit, take Japan gold-size, with which hatch and lay it over with gold-dust; and if your judgment and experience will allow of it, you may touch and heighten all the strongest lights, and deepen your shadows too on the forside, which gives so much life to it, that Limners themselves have been deceived, and mistook it for a piece of real painting. I desire young beginners to forbear, and not attempt this way of finishing, till experience and practice shall give them incouragement. If you design to varnish and polish any of these Prints, lay on the colours without skins, and very even on the backside, and permit them to drie at least a week (for the longer the better) before you offer to varnish them after this following manner.

To

To varnish these Prints, or other Pictures, without polishing.

Take of the beſt white Japan-varniſh, and an equal quantity of
Varniſh made of Maſtick and oyl of Turpentine; into theſe ming-
led together, dip a fine Camels-hair-bruſh, and with it varniſh o-
ver your piece, four or five times carefully by the fire, as you
are taught to do Japan; and you'l find that it gives a very rich
gloſs.

To varniſh pictures, and poliſh them, like Japan.

With white-Japan-varniſh only waſh over your work five or ſix
times, obſerving all the method for Japan directly. When it has
reſted three or four days, lay the Picture on the Cuſhion,
whereon you cut the Leaf-gold: then with Tripole and water
poliſh it; and laſtly, clear it up as you do White-Japan.

Theſe are the Rules in ſhort, I thought fit to lay down in-
the treatiſe of this pretty Art; and I queſtion not but they are
full, moſt exact, and ſatisfactory, and will be found ſo, when the
Ingenious Ladies ſhall put them into practice.

To Imitate and counterfeit
TORTOISE-SHELL *and* MARBLE.

CHAP. XXVI.

BEfore Japan was made in England, the imitation of Tortoiſe-
ſhell was much in requeſt, for Cabinets, Tables, and the like;
but we being greedy of Novelty, made theſe give way to modern
Inventions: not, but that tis ſtill in vogue, and fancied by many,
for Glaſs-frames, and ſmall Boxes; nay, Houſe-Painters have of
late frequently endeavoured it, for Battens, and Mouldings of
Rooms; but I muſt of neceſſity ſay, with ſuch ill ſucceſs, that I
have not to the beſt of my remembrance met with any that have
humour'd the Shell ſo far, as to make it look either natural, or
delightful. But, to avoid all reflections, I muſt attribute this to
that miſtaken piece of frugality in them, who think, if they can
agree with a Painter by the greatt, their buſineſs is done; for by

these means, they not allowing the Artist a Living price, he cannot
spend both his oyl and labour, nor stretch his performances to the
utmost extent of his skill.   On the other hand, some there be who
are indeed willing, but not being Masters of what they profess, sink
and come short through their inabilities.   I believe the complaint
is universal ; the ingenious and most excellent in each profession,
being destitute of a reward that is answerable and proportioned to
the worthiness of his undertaking.

But tis high time that we close with the business in hand.   And
first, the Tortoise-shell, I propose for your imitation, is that which is
laid upon Silver-Foil, and is always made use of for Cabinets and
Boxes, for it gives life and beauty to the Shell, which else would
appear dull and heavy.   Now to counterfeit this very well ; your
wood ought to be close-grain'd, smooth, and cleanly wrought off,
as Pear-tree, but if it be a coarse-grained wood, as Deal, Oak, or
the like, you must prime it with Whiting, as you have been taught
in the chapter of black Japan for coarse-grained woods.   When
either of these are rushed smooth, as is required , take a fit varnishing tool dipt into a gallipot of the thickest of your Seed-lac-varnish, and wet with this varnish the breadth of a Silver-leaf, which
you must take up with cotton, and clap on it whilst tis moist, dab-
bing it close to the work, as you have been taught in Guilding.
This done, wash again, and lay on another leaf of Silver, ordering
it as before, and so continue, till the whole is so overspread with
Silver.   When tis through drie, with a fine hair-brush sweep off
all the loose Silver.   Next, grind Collins-earth very finely on a
grinding-stone, mixed either with common size, or gum-water ;
this I esteem better than Lamblack, because Collins-earth comes
much nearer to the colour of the Shell : Being finely ground,
mix it with more common size, or gum-water, as you have made
use of either in the grinding.   With this spot the darkest of your
Shell, striving to the utmost to imitate it as nearly as tis possible ;
and in order hereunto, I counsel you to procure a piece or more of
the true, right Shell, that hath much variety in it ; this lying by
you, will quicken and assist your fancie, and enable you to perform
it with much more ease and cunning.   You may observe, (when
this is done, that several reds, lighter and darker, offer themselves
to view on the edges of the black, and sometimes lie in streaks on
the transparent part of the shell : To imitate this, you must grind
Sanguis Draconis very fine with gum-water ; and with a small pencil draw those warm reds, flushing it in and about the dark places
more thick, but fainter, thinner, and with less colour towards the
lighter parts of the shells ; sweetning it so, that by degrees it may
loose its strength of red, being intermixt with, and quite lost in
the silver, or more transparent part. Tis worthy your observation, that those who are expert and ready at spotting or working
this imitation, do usually grind the forementioned colours drie and
very

very finely upon a ftone, and mix 'em with fine Lace-varnifh as they work them, which is moft agreeable and proper, as I have noted before, being not fo apt to polifh off as Size or gum-water; notwithftanding, I advife young beginners to ufe fize or gumwater, for I fuppofe they are not able to do it fo well, that it fhould not require a review and correction; for then they may with eafe and a little care rub out any faulty place, and go over it again, until tis done artificially, (but this convenience is not to be had, if you imploy Lace-varnifh at the firft.) When this is done, and dried, give it fix wafhes of your Seed-lace-varnifh; let it reft one day; after which time rufh it gently, till tis fmooth and fit for the fecond operation : in order to which, grind Dragons-blood and Gambogium, in an equal, but fmall quantity, very finely; put them into as much Seed-lace-varnifh as will wafh it fix times more : permit it to ftand twelve hours, and then allow it the third varnifhing, and with the laft mixture wafh it fo often, till your filver is changed into gold, or a colour like it. Note, that your firft wafhings may be with the coarfe, the two laft with the fine and cleareft of your Seed-lace-varnifh; avoid making your varnifh too thick and high coloured with Gambogium, and Sanguis Draconis, but heighten it by degrees, otherwife your filver will be too high-coloured, before you have given it a fufficient body of varnifh. When it has ftood two days, polifh and clear it up, as you have been inftructed in the treatife of black varnifhing.

Another way to counterfeit Tortoife-fhell.

First, prime, lacker, and fize your work in oyl very thin, as you are taught before in the Art of Guilding , and when your filver is laid on and dried, let thefe colours be ground fine and thick in drying-oyl, placing them on your Pallet ; they are, burnt Umber, Collins-earth, brown Pink, and Lake. Do over your work with Turpentine-varnifh, and whilft it is wet, mix brown Pink and Lake thin with varnifh ; and lay all your fainteft clouds or fpots, which you may foften very fweetly, feeing your varnifh is moift. After three hours ftanding , or longer , if the colours are drie, with a large, foft Tool, pafs it lightly over ; and again wetting it, lay in your clouds more warm and dark with Umber and Collins-earth, before tis drie ; always obferving the life, and fweetning your work, which is blending and mixing two colours after they are laid, fo that you cannot perceive where either of them begin or end, but infenfibly join with each other. If the clouds are not dark enough, repeat the varnifhing and clouding once more, where tis required. When tis well dried, glaze it two or three times with brown Pink, yet a little tincture of Verdegreas in it will not be amif; if you had rather, you may varnifh it with Lace-varnifh, and finifh it as you did the former.

To

Whiten and prepare your wood in all respects as you do for white Japan; and after you have done it over with flake white, or white-lead, if you defign a white with some veins, use some Vine-black, (which is made of the cuttings of Vines burnt and grinded,) mix two or three degrees of it with white-lead and a very weak fize being warmed, until you have produced the intended colour for the clouds and veins of the Marble. Being thus far advanc't, call for a large, clean brush, wet your piece' over with water, and before tis dry, with a great Camels-hair-pencil, dipt in the palest thin mixture, flush or lay the faintest large clouds and veins of your Marble, which being laid on whilst the work is wet, will lie fo soft and sweet, that the original will not exceed it. Then if your work be not too drie, take a smaller pencil, and with a colour one degree darker than the first, touch all the lesser veins and variety of the Marble: If your work drie too fast, wet it again with the brush and water, and lay not on your colours when the water is running off, lest they bear it company. Lastly, take a small-pointed feather, and with the deepest colour touch and break all your fuddain or smaller veins, irregular, wild, and confused, as you have them in the natural Marble. After a days drying, cold-clear it, that is, do it over with Ifinglafs or Parchment-fize; and then var-nish, polish, and clear it up, exactly in all things according to the directions for white Japan, to which places, and others above men-tioned, we refer you. By mixing other colours this way, any fort of Marble is fubject to your imitation; and, if neatly done, well polisht, and varnisht, will not only exceed any Marbling in oyl, but will in beauty and glofs equal the real ftone.

CHAP. XXVII.

Of Dying or Staining Wood, Ivory, &c.

To Dye Wood a beautiful Red.

VVoods, that are very white, take this dye the beft of any: fet a kettle of water boiling with a handful of Allom, caft your wood into it, permitting it to boil a little; that done, take your wood out, and put into the faid water two handfuls of Brafil wood, then return your wood into the veffel again to boil for a quarter of an hour, and tis concluded. When dry, you may rush and polish it, or varnish it with the tops of Seed-lacc-varnish, and polish it; by which management, you will find the wood covered with a rich and beautiful colour.

To ftain a fine Yellow.

Take Burr or knotty Afh, or any other wood that is white, cur-led, and knotty; fmooth and rush it very well, and having warmed
it

it, with a brush dipt in Aqua fortis wash over the wood, and hold
it to the fire, as you do Japan-work, until it leaves smoaking, when
dry rush it again, for the Aqua fortis will make it very rough. If
to these you add a polish, and varnish it with Seed-lacc, and then
again polish it, you'l find no outlandish wood surpass it; for the
curled and knotty parts admit of so much variety, being in some
places hard, in others soft and open-grained, to which Aqua fortis
gives a deeper colour, than to the harder and more resisting parts.
In short, you'l perceive a pleasing variety interwoven, beyond what
you could imagine or expect. If you put filings or bits of metals,
as brass, copper, and iron, into the Aqua fortis, each metal will
produce a different tincture: the best French Pistols are stockt generally with this sort of wood, and stained after this manner.

To Dye or Stain Woods of any colour, for Inlaid or Flower'd work, done by the Cabinet-makers.

Use the moistest horse-dung you can get, that has been made the
night before; through a sieve or cloath squeez out what moisture
you judge sufficient for the purpose, convey it into several small
vessels fit for the design; in each of these dissolve of Roach-allom,
and Gum Arabick, the bigness of a nutmeg, and with them mix
reds, blews, greens, or what colours best please you, suffering them
to stand two or three days, yet not without often stirring them.
Then take your woods (of which I think Pear-tree is the best if't be
white,) cut them as thick as an half-crown, which is in all reason
thick enough for any Fineered or Inlaid work, and of what bredth
you please; making your liquors or colours boiling hot, put the
wood into it, for as long time as will sufficiently colour them, yet
some must be taken out sooner than the rest, by which means you'l
have different shades of the same colour; for the longer they lie
in, the higher and deeper will be the colours: and such variety you
may well imagin contributes much to the beauty and neatness of
the work, and agrees with the nature of your parti-coloured flowers.

To Dye or Stain Wood Black.

Take Log-wood, and boil it in water or vinegar, and whilst very
hot brush or stain over your wood with it two or three times; then
take the Galls, and Copperas, well beaten, and boil them well in
water, with which wash or stain your work so often till it be a
black to your mind; the oftner it is layed, the better will your
black be: if your work be small enough, you may steep it in your
liquors instead of washing it.

The best Black Dye for Ivory, Horn, Bone, &c.

Put pieces of Brass into Aqua fortis, letting it stand till tis turned green, with which wash your Ivory (being polished) once or
twice. Next, boil Logwood in water, into which put your Ivory,
whilst tis warm, and in a little time it gives a fine black, which
you

you muſt now ruſh and poliſh again, and twill have as good a gloſs and black as any Japan or Ebony.

If you deſire any foldage, flowers, or the like fancies ſhould remain white, and of the ſame colour with the Ivory; draw them neatly on the Ivory with Turpentine varniſh, before you ſtain it; for thoſe places which you touch with the varniſh, are ſo ſecured by it, that the Dye cannot approach or diſcolour them. After tis dyed, if you can hatch and ſhadow thoſe fancies with a Graver, and fill the lines by rubbing and clearing up the whole with Lamblack and Oyl, it may add much to its ornament and perfection.

To Stain a Green colour on Wood, Ivory, Horn, or Bones.

Firſt, prepare either of them in Allom-water, by boiling them well in it, as you were juſt now inſtructed. Afterwards grind of Spaniſh-green, or thick common Verdegreas, a reaſonable quantity, with half as much Sal-Armoniack; then put them into the ſtrongeſt wine-vinegar, together with the wood, keeping it hot over the fire till tis green enough: if the wood is too large, then waſh it over ſcalding hot, as in the other inſtances.

To Dye Ivory. &c, Red.

Put quick-lime into rain-water for a night; ſtrain the clear through a cloath, and to every pint of water add half an ounce of the ſcrapings of Braſil-wood: having firſt boil'd it in Allom-water, then boil it in this, till tis red enough to pleaſe you.

Thus, Courteous Reader, are we at lengthth arriv'd at our deſired Port. Our Performances have been no way inferiour to our Promiſes. What we ingaged for in the beginning, we have punctually accompliſht; and nothing certainly remains, but that you convert our Precepts to Practice; for that will be the ready way to examin, and try, whether they are falſe or inſufficient. We have all along been directed by an unerring Guide, Experience; and do therefore adviſe you, upon the leaſt miſcarriage, to make a diligent review, and doubt not but ſecond thoughts will convince you of too ſlight an obſervance. We deſire you'd be as exact and regular in your performances, as we have been in ours; for by theſe means, Satisfaction will attend both Parties, all our deſigns muſt ſucceed to our wiſh, and our Labours ſhall be crowned with ſucceſs and reputation.

FINIS.

The Lid of a Powder Box

The Lid of a Patch Box

The Side of a Patch Box

The Side of the Powder Box

The Fellow to it

The Fellow to it

i

The Sides

The Sides

The Follow

The Follow

Other patterns for Pewter Boxes

Other Patterns for Patch Boxes 3

For the Dus of Patch Boxes

Another Sort of work for yᵉ Sides of Patch Boxes

The fellow to it

The fellow to it

Cloth
Brushes

Combs
Brushes

A Pincushing Trunks for Pendents Necklace Rings & Jewell:~

The Top of a 12 Inch Frame for a Looking Glass for Jappan Worke

The Bottom of y.^e Same frame

The Side of y.^e frame on y.^e Right han.^d

The Side of y.^e frame on y.^e Left han.^d

The topp of a halfe Round Frame for Japan worke, called a ne Irish Dreſing frame for a Looking Glaſs

The Bottom of ye ſaid Frame

The Side of ye frame to ye Right hand

The Side of ye Frame to ye Left hand

12

A Pagod Worshipp'
in ÿ Indies

Another

22

23

An Embassy

www.ingramcontent.com/pod-product-compliance
Lightning Source LLC
Chambersburg PA
CBHW030603270326
41927CB00007B/1033